In the sweetness of friendship let there be laughter, and sharing of pleasures. For in the dew of little things the heart finds its morning and is refreshed.

Khalil Gibran

The Friendship Book

A THOUGHT FOR EACH DAY | 2020

The Friendship Book

A NEW Year just beginning
Who knows what lies ahead?
Will there be love and laughter
Along the path we tread?

Will there be friends we've yet to meet
And happiness to find?
Forgetting last year's problems,
We'll leave them all behind.

Will there be new excitement,
A time when dreams come true?
Step out toward tomorrow now;
It waits for me and you!

Iris Hesselden

January

AUTHORS like to begin a book with an exciting first page. After that, they lay out the premise of the story. Next comes a series of set-backs and achievements, excitingly described, until a satisfying conclusion is reached.

The English poet Edith Lovejoy Pierce once described the year in a similar way:

"We will open the book. Its pages are blank. We are going to put words on them ourselves. The book is called Opportunity, and its first chapter is New Year's Day."

If you make any resolutions, lay them out on page one. Don't expect the keeping of them to be easy. Your story will have ups and downs. But understand, this "book" will take a year to complete.

Write the year in such a way that when it comes time to "close the book", you can sit back and know you made the very best of your year of Opportunity.

THE playwright J.B. Priestley once filled a book with things that delighted him. Each item (and his response to it) was entertainingly described over two or three pages of the book – except for number seventy-four.

In just four lines, he told how, on dark nights and from a particular room in his house, he could see the lights of three different lighthouses.

Why was that delightful? He didn't know. It just was.

Unexplainable delights. They might just be the most delightful of all, don't you think?

Friday — January 3

L OOK *with new eyes*
On everyday things.
See what delight
Doing this brings.

The bright changing sky,
Great waves and sea foam,
The lights of a town,
The road back to home.

And most of all look
With renewed love and pleasure
At the faces of loved ones:
All gifts beyond measure.

Elizabeth Horrocks

Saturday — January 4

D ID your resolutions this year focus outward, on material things, or inwards, to the kind of person you might like to be?

The kind of person we are is, in part, determined by our will-power and our intentions. But other people, and our circumstances, often play important roles in determining the end result.

But the attributes that are most easily shaped by outside influences tend to be the more superficial ones. The essential traits in a personality tend to be more straightforward – and teams of horses usually couldn't alter them.

What sort of traits am I talking about?

Well, the Roman Emperor and Stoic philosopher Marcus Aurelius thought it vitally important that it should "not be in any man's power to say truly of thee that thou art not simple or that thou art not good."

Simplicity and goodness. Traits, I imagine, that a very fine life could be built upon. And the best thing about them? As the Emperor/philosopher said, "Who is he that shall hinder thee from being simple or good?"

No-one!

A perfect day for cloud-watching.

Padang Padang Beach, Bali.

IN 2017 a buyer paid four hundred and fifty million pounds for a painting by Leonardo da Vinci, making it the most expensive painting ever.

So, what did it depict, this wonderfully expensive piece of art?

Jesus Christ, the greatest gift the world has ever known. The greatest free gift!

Da Vinci was a genius. His paintings are exquisite, and rare. In a world that values such things, perhaps the price tag is merited.

But, oh, that we lived in a world where his gifts – love, understanding, sacrifice, patience, forgiveness and life – were valued as highly.

Monday — January 6

HOW much effort would you put into searching for hidden treasure?

Commenting on how difficult life could be, physicist and chemist Marie Curie said, "What of it?" She went on, saying, "We must believe that we are gifted for something, and that this thing, at whatever cost, must be attained."

Your gift to the world? It's worth a little effort to uncover!

Tuesday — January 7

AN Arab proverb declares, "All men are but the teeth of a comb." I confess when I heard that I remembered past combs of mine that were missing many teeth and thought the proverb meant we were easily detached. Then I thought again.

I imagined what an obstacle a head of tangled hair must seem to a comb. But it gets the job done; those tangles are untangled, the unruly is brought to order. Each tooth on the comb does its bit.

The teeth of a comb? It's not such a glamorous description. But if it means standing side by side with my brothers and sisters to get done a job that would be impossible for any of us on our own, then I'll take that!

HARRY laid a dozen matches on a metal tray. They were all the same way up and there was just a small gap between each of them.

"Watch this!" he said, as he picked up the first match and struck it.

It flared, and he laid it back on the tray. The first match lit the second. The second match lit the third. The third match lit the fourth. You know where this is going.

But, with the point of a pencil, he pushed the fifth match out of the line.

The first four matches burned and shrivelled until the flames went out. The fifth one – and the remaining matches – remained untouched.

"Sometimes," Harry began, "no matter how tempting it might be to join in with all the fuss – the latest fight or argument – it is best just to take yourself out of there.

"For your own sake, and the sake of everyone else who might get caught up in it, too."

MILLIONS of people will have gone for a hike through America's national parks since they were established. John Muir, the Scots-born naturalist who helped set them up, would have objected to me saying that.

Why? Because he disliked the word "hike". His preferred word was "saunter".

He once explained that travellers to the Holy Land in the Middle Ages would often be asked where they were going, and they might reply, "À la sainte terre" – to the Holy Land. They became known as "sainte terre-ers" or "saunterers".

Mr Muir believed the mountains of America – being part of the greater Creation – were no more or less holy than the Holy Land. Thus, they should be, reverently, sauntered through rather than hiked.

With that in mind, where would you like to saunter today?

SOME time before the publication in 1924 of "The Thirty-nine Steps", John Buchan, the author, compiled a book of his favourite Scottish poetry.

In his introduction to "The Northern Muse" he wrote, "I have made this little anthology with no other purpose than to please myself."

Yet a copy of it sits by my bedside almost a century later. I have taken much pleasure from it in the still of these long, dark evenings before falling asleep.

Those who create beauty – or even present it – cannot get away with claiming selfish motives. They may have shaped it a little, or pointed it in a certain direction, but beauty, once set free, goes where it likes and gives pleasure to whomever it will.

I am sure Mr Buchan knew that, and I thank him.

Saturday — January 11

GREATER love hath no man than this, that a man lay down his life for his friends."

That's undoubtedly true.

But I saw a woman sit herself down on a wet pavement recently, so that a hurt and crying older woman she had never met before could rest against her and be comforted until an ambulance arrived.

That's pretty great, too, if you ask me.

Sunday — January 12

AT a time of looking forwards, and also of nostalgia, we must remember we live in the present.

George MacDonald, the great 19th-century Scottish preacher and writer, reminds us that God exists throughout time and that, when we "do our work in the great present" we can leave "both past and future to Him, to whom they are ever present."

A little night-time reading.

Monday — January 13

THESE shorter January days reminded me of a friend who thought himself a philosopher.

He once told me, "The brighter the light, the darker the shadow. We each have both within us."

I am sure he was making some profound point about balance, good and bad, yin and yang, etc.

I should have paid more attention, but his words took my mind in a different direction.

It is a wonderful thing, I thought, and one of the most beautiful aspects of human nature, that people living under a dark shadow can still, through their love and determination, be a bright light for others.

Shine, my friends. You are appreciated!

Tuesday — January 14

INSPIRATION can strike at the oddest times.

In this instance, I was babysitting. While the little princess watched Disney's live-action "Cinderella" on DVD, I did some tidying up.

That's when I heard Cinderella's mother say, "Have courage, and be kind."

They seem very different things – courage and kindness. Kindness is so often seen as the soft option, something only the weak need concern themselves with.

In a world that encourages us to think that way (because it would be irrevocably changed if people thought any differently) it often asks a lot of us to put others first – or to be seen to put others first.

Sometimes, appearing callous or careless – as the world would encourage us to be – is actually the weak option. But we can always do better than that, be kinder than that, if we only have courage.

Have courage and be kind.

It's the best way I know to find a happy ever after for everyone.

A FRIEND had told the Lady of the House a name. When I asked for it later, in connection with something else, she knew she had heard it but she couldn't remember it.

"Weren't you paying attention?" I asked, perhaps a little brusquely as my mind was on the other matter.

"She told me at the coffee shop," my sweetheart replied. "And remembering isn't what those chats are about. In fact, that might almost be a betrayal of trust.

"The important thing is to let each other get it out there; to lay the burden down amongst friends for a while. Remembering what was said is of purely secondary importance."

Then, seeing my completely baffled expression, she shook her head.

There was more than a little pity in that expression.

The male world and the female world are surely two very different places, but I am so glad they exist alongside each other. And that we get to visit from time to time.

A DAM MAKOS, in his book "A Higher Call", records a conversation between two World War II German pilots.

One had just disabled a Soviet plane. The Russian, believing he would be shot if he did so, refused to bail out. The German flyer drew up alongside his opponent's plane and signalled that it was safe to "take to the silk".

His friend and fellow ace asked him why he took such a dangerous risk.

He replied, "You must remember that, one day, that Russian pilot was the baby son of a beautiful Russian girl. He has his right to life and love the same as we do."

Reading that, I wondered how we might treat even the most troublesome individual if we took the time to think of them as they once were – as we all once were – a babe in arms?

Friday — January 17

YESTERDAY we had rain. Later, it turned to sleet for a while. Then it stopped. During the night, the temperature dipped.

This morning, the sky was clear and the sun shone brightly.

All of which meant that, as I walked the dog, I stepped around long blades of grass bedecked by, and bowed by the weight of, thousands of frozen dewdrops. The field looked like it had been liberally spread with diamonds.

As I watched a crystal-clear dewdrop melt on my palm, I reflected on all it took to produce such an exquisite thing.

May the times of difficult "weather" in our lives have a similar, purifying, beautifying effect.

Saturday — January 18

LES NICHOL never went to South Africa. But the Ndebele-speaking people of South Africa have a saying I am sure he would have liked.

"Zidele amathambo" means, "Give yourself up, bones as well."

When I asked him how he crossed the turbulent winter streams during his years as a shepherd, he replied, "I threw my jacket across first. I only have the one jacket."

Bones and all. Jacket and all. We have this one life. Live it for all it's worth.

Sunday — January 19

IT was a radio discussion on dry-stone walling.

One waller mentioned "dressing" a stone, by which she meant knocking rough edges off until it fitted. A second expert said that in his part of the country they never dressed the stones.

The first agreed, saying the time spent doing that was generally wasted time and, after all, "We are in the business of fitting imperfect things into a cohesive whole."

Imperfect things? A cohesive whole? I'd no idea church and dry-stone walling had so much in common!

Monday — January 20

I HAVE often heard it said that kindness is its own reward. And there is definitely a warm feeling that comes with doing someone a good turn, even if no-one else ever knows about it.

But I have never heard a decent explanation for that feeling, until one Good Samaritan said, "It's as though my soul just told me, 'This is how you are supposed to feel all the time!'"

That's surely worth repeated reminders!

Tuesday — January 21

H OW to keep on being cheerful, when often one is not,
I thought was quite impossible, except that I forgot
That, when my mind is active, and I am busy, too,
Time flies by so quickly, whatever task I do.
I sing myself a happy tune, the liveliest I know,
And soon my work is finished, although I might be slow.
So if sadness visits unannounced, and knocks upon my door,
I don't get all frustrated or downhearted any more.
I turn my back the other way,
And turn another page,
And sadness leaves quite quickly
When I tell him, "I'm engaged!"

Dawn Lawrence

Wednesday — January 22

I LONG to accomplish a great and noble task," Helen Keller once wrote.

And I long to write an epic novel that will hold a mirror to society and turn it in a more civilised direction.

"But it is my chief duty," Ms Keller continued, "to accomplish small tasks as if they were great and noble."

So I decided to write a cheerful letter to a struggling friend instead.

Thursday — January 23

BARRY MANILOW has been a big name in show-biz for over 40 years. There can't be many talk shows he hasn't appeared on.

I recently heard him talking to J.P. Devlin on Radio 4 and he came across as a lovely person. Then, at the end, he said, "I've never had an interview quite like this. You were wonderful!"

Devlin's colleagues tried jokingly to make it seem like Manilow said that to everyone. Perhaps he does. But if he does, wouldn't that make him an even nicer person?

You can make someone's day with a few words. Some people don't bother. Some people bother all the time!

Friday — January 24

THE world knows Roald Dahl as the very successful author of children's books like "Matilda", and "Charlie And The Chocolate Factory". But he was also a fighter pilot in WWII, a diplomat and an intelligence officer.

You could say he knew a thing or two about people, and his opinions might be worth paying a little attention to.

When asked what he liked in others, he replied, "I think probably kindness is my number one attribute in a human being. I'll put it before any of the things like courage, or bravery, or generosity, or anything else."

Saturday — January 25

DO you remember snow globes? You shook them and tiny flakes of "snow" filled the painted scene. Pretty.

But who likes being shaken like that?

Life often gives us a shake.

But, of course, once you sat the globe down, the snow began to settle.

Don't play the agitation game. Sit. Settle. Be still.

Reclaim your peace, and your life.

Sunday — January 26

CONTENTMENT! What a gift it must be.

Edward Bouverie Pusey, a 19th-century English churchman, had a recipe for it.

Don't complain, he advised, not even about the weather.

Never imagine yourself in situations you aren't; don't compare whatever you have with whatever another has; don't waste time wishing this had happened, or that hadn't happened.

Above all, remember "God Almighty loves thee better and more wisely than thou dost thyself."

That last "ingredient" we can surely all find contentment in.

Monday — January 27

WE left New Year behind us,
Resolutions laid aside,
And now we're on a journey
With hope to be our guide.
The winter may seem endless,
Yet just below the earth
So many seeds awaiting
The moment of their birth.
So greet each new tomorrow,
Be cheerful, come what may,
For just around the corner
Spring is on the way!

Iris Hesselden

Tuesday — January 28

IF ever I feel too far past the full flush of youth, I console myself with the words of the 17th-century poet, Edmund Waller.

"The soul's dark cottage, batter'd and decay'd,
Lets in new light through chinks that time has made."

The new light is beautiful and well worth the many chinks!

LEGEND has it that Socrates learned to dance when he was seventy. Why? Because he felt an important part of himself had been neglected.

Now, I am too much of a gentleman to ask your age, but I am more than happy to ask both of us the question the great philosopher must have asked himself. That being, "What important thing (or things) have I neglected thus far in my life?"

Not always an easy question. But I do believe that once we ask it – and answer it – we might feel like dancing, too.

Thursday — January 30

HAVE you ever watched a live stream? Modern technology means you can watch events unfold, or listen to lectures being given, anywhere in the world. You "stream" them via the internet.

Now, have you ever watched a real stream?

One might be more educational; one might be better for your soul. You decide which is which.

Friday — January 31

HAVE you heard of the statue that hitch-hiked across America? No, I didn't dream it! A sculptor carved a four-feet-tall statue of a hitch-hiking boy, complete with the traditional thumb in the air. Then he left it by a Californian roadside, with his parents' address on a sign hung around the boy's neck.

Several weeks later the wooden boy arrived on another sidewalk, outside his final destination – in Connecticut! A series of kind strangers, on various journeys, had transported him two-and-a-half thousand miles. To no benefit for themselves. Just to help someone they had never met.

I'm not recommending hitch-hiking as a means of getting about, but I am saying there is far more kindness in the world than we could ever imagine.

Just ask the hitch-hiking boy!

A babbling brook.

Olympic Peninsula, Washington State.

February

PETE tutors a creative writing group. He was recently enthusing about a sonnet one of the members of his group had come up with.

"I couldn't have written anything half as beautiful," he told me, shaking his head in admiration.

I had a notion he had said the same thing on other occasions.

"Do you ever think, perhaps, some of the people coming up with such great writing – writing you admit you couldn't do – ought to be running the group instead of you?" I asked him as gently as I could.

He looked puzzled for a second, then he grinned.

"Nope!" he replied. "They might be better writers, but I'm the better encourager. The two things might be connected, don't you think?"

Where would we be without the encouragers?

GEORGE is no evangelist, but the minister says he brings more people to church than anyone.

George is the church gardener, which means he is outside throughout every season of the year. On wet days, people commiserate with him. On sunny days, folk are happy to chat over the wall.

"Once we discover we have the weather in common," George says, "chat soon turns to what else we share. Our blessing, like. And one thing leads to another."

The rain and God's love. Things we all have in common!

Monday — February 3

A STOIC philosopher went in search of strength, something I am sure we could all do with a little more of. He finally came to the conclusion that "You have power over your mind – not outside events. Realise this and you will find strength."

Oh, and did I mention his name? He was Marcus Aurelius, Emperor of Rome, and the most powerful man in the world.

Tuesday — February 4

SOMETIMES life's hard going,
The way can seem so tough,
Yet our Saviour promises
He'll give us strength enough.
Though the road ahead is hidden,
The Good Lord knows the way,
He guides us and directs us,
Through each brand-new day.
So remember as we journey
We don't journey on our own,
Jesus walks beside us
So we'll never walk alone.

Amanda-Jayne Lanceley

Wednesday — February 5

HEROD the Great, Catherine the Great, Alexander the Great . . . all those other Greats. Judged by their power and influence – the usual standards of the world – they deserved their titles.

But the Lebanese poet and wise man, Kahlil Gibran, suggested another standard.

"He alone is great who turns the voice of the wind into a song made sweeter by his own loving."

Adding to the beauty of the world might not get you a place in history books. You'll never get that title attached to your name.

But it takes a great heart to want to do such a thing in the first place. And the world will be greater because you did it.

Thursday — February 6

WHAT do you think of when you hear the term "the age of chivalry"? Knights in armour? Damsels in distress?

Whatever springs to mind, I imagine it belongs to a time long past.

Charles Kingsley, author of "The Water-Babies", wrote, "The age of chivalry is never past, so long as there is a wrong left unredressed on earth."

The age of chivalry lies in the past. But it could also be our future, if we would have it so.

Friday — February 7

YOU see things like that on Facebook," the man said to me. "But you never expect them to happen to you in real life."

Really? I suppose. But why don't we?

We do see good stuff online, in films or on TV; things we wish would happen to us; things we know would go on to make the world a better place.

Having seen them, we have a choice. We can wait for them to happen to us in real life, or we can go out and make them happen for others, and set an example that might easily come back to us!

We shouldn't rely on the movies, or Facebook, for those special moments. We can always write our own scripts.

Saturday — February 8

I NEVER experienced Great-aunt Louisa's "Quiet Hours". The Lady of the House tells me they happened once a month. Friends who felt the need of some peace would sit around the fire, silently allowing the time to pass. When the last grain of sand had slipped through the hour-glass, hugs and thanks would be exchanged, then everyone would head home.

Those were much less hectic times, but still those hours were appreciated.

Like I said, Great-aunt Louisa's "Quiet Hours" were no part of my experience, but I seem to benefit even from the thought of them.

A warming drink by the fire.

Sunday — February 9

ONE of my favourite times of the day – especially at this time of the year – is the moment, after a dog-walk, when I loosen my mucky boots, leave them on the rack to dry and finally put my slippers on.

It never fails to remind me of these tongue-in-cheek words by Goethe: "We must always change, renew, rejuvenate ourselves, so that we don't become stick-in-the-muds."

And it is so very muddy out there!

Monday — February 10

LARRY and I have different political views. I have almost fallen out with him over them.

Then I remember he loves his wife, he is a good father and a fun grandad. His neighbours are glad to live next door to him, and through his church he regularly feeds the hungry and helps the dispossessed.

But I would fall out with him over politics? What a nonsense!

As the preacher and writer George MacDonald once said, "It is amazing from what a mere fraction of a fact concerning him a man will dare judge the whole of another man."

Tuesday — February 11

IN times of hunger and hardship, a man was offered good farm land in exchange for one of his seven children.

When he and his wife discussed it, there was one child too dear to her, one too dear to him, one was still a baby, one was too much help to spare and one who would not stand to be parted from another. Then there was the wayward son – the one who gave them the most trouble.

Mother and father decided no other would love him – and he was the one who needed love the most. So they did without the farm and kept their family.

May we be as generous to those who most need our love.

Wednesday — February 12

SOMEONE suggested that discoveries are only things that were always there, but now we see them!

Think of all the discoveries made in all the different fields of human enquiry, in the history of mankind. Yet all of those things were there from the beginning.

What else might we not be seeing?

Personally, I am hoping the next big discovery has to do with understanding the true power of love and its amazing potential to change the world.

It's always been there! May we learn to see it.

Thursday — February 13

I HAVE been present several times when people (on the receiving end of his kindnesses) have told Harry, "You didn't have to do that!"

His usual response sometimes surprises folk.

"If I had to do it," he tells them gruffly, "I wouldn't."

And that's that.

He likes a bit of mystery, does Harry, so I have never asked him what he means by that.

But I do know that it's what a man or woman does when they don't have to do anything that is the true measure of their character. Not what they have to do.

Friday — February 14

DID you know that Valentine's Day is known as "Friend's Day" in Finland? Or that in Guatemala it's the "Day Of Love And Friendship"?

I am not going to suggest we focus more on friends here. But I believe that the secret of real happiness does lie in ensuring that our sweethearts are also our best friends.

Don't you agree?

A garden in flower.

Saturday — February 15

JAMES BALLANTINE worked on the stained-glass windows in the House of Lords in the 1800s. He saw power and wealth up close.

His impression of them might be guessed at from his poem "Ilka Blade O' Grass Keps Its Ain Drap O' Dew". In those lines he points out that, even in the driest of times, "the genial night, wi' balmy breath" brings to every blade of grass its own drop of dew to see it through the day.

Power and wealth might be all very well, but they are often questionably achieved and hard to keep. Whereas, if our needs are simple, every blade of grass – every one of us – will be provided for.

Sunday — February 16

IN the 11th-century Japanese novel "The Tale Of Genji", October is called "The Godless Month". I'm not sure what the climate is like in Japan in October. Maybe it's as bleak as February in the UK. But any gardener will tell you Mother Nature spends half of winter preparing for spring. Some seeds are already at work; they just haven't broken the surface yet.

There are no such things as godless months, although there may be times that seem devoid of God's presence. But that's when the ground-work gets done. In reality, there are simply times of preparation, and times of flowering.

Monday — February 17

*W*HEN *you meet that special someone, life begins anew,*
The ordinary seems beautiful and the sky is brighter blue.
The sun's a little warmer, and everything seems right;
Your time together's precious and you hate to say goodnight.
The music that is playing when you dance becomes "your song";
A hand in theirs feels wonderful, your heart says you belong.
So if you have a love like that please handle it with care;
Don't let the years diminish it or break the bond you share,
For love is like a flower needing nourishment to live,
So shower it with warmth, and all the kindness you can give.

Linda Brown

29

Tuesday — February 18

IN the shorter days our moods often grow duller.

Albert Camus, the philosopher, had a quick and easy solution for the situation.

"Find meaning," he wrote. "Distinguish melancholy from sadness."

"How?" you might ask.

"Go for a walk," would be his reply.

Let the wind blow the cobwebs away; let the rain wash you clean; let the cold bring colour to your cheeks. If you can, go for a walk!

Wednesday — February 19

HAVE you ever heard anyone say they were educated at the School of Hard Knocks?

It's a joke. But it inspired a thought.

I would much rather be educated by soft touches, by gentle hints, by a wise word at the right time, by a word not said, or the guidance of one who had travelled the road before.

Anyone can learn from hard knocks, but those who grow and develop through subtler influences and hints really are paying attention at school.

Thursday — February 20

THE Lady of the House and I had gone on a winter break. But winter, as it has a habit of doing, delayed our return journey.

Hearing of our plight, my friend Fran said, "The journey home should always be smooth. It should be a law."

It was an off-the-cuff remark, but it stayed with me. Can there be any place more special than home? And shouldn't we all offer, and expect to receive, all the help there is in getting there?

Thankfully, we found plenty of new friends willing to help us. May we be as good a help to those we meet on their travels. After all, aren't we all, ultimately, just journeying home?

Friday — February 21

AMIDST the hustle and bustle of modern life, the words of Chinese philosopher Lin Yutang might be of use.

"Beside the noble art of getting things done," he wrote, "there is the noble art of leaving things undone."

Wisdom lies in eliminating the non-essentials!

Saturday — February 22

IN the 1900s, a man set out to compile a volume of traditional songs. It involved travelling, and everyone he met had an opinion on his work. What qualified as "traditional" and which lyrics were original were hotly contested topics, and discussed at great length.

He mentioned the naysayers in the preface, but he thanked those whose heartening words had been "like water to the tired and thirsty traveller". He added that "they refreshed and gladdened the heart of the collector and lightened up for him the path of the daily pilgrimage, when otherwise it might have seemed naught but a gloomy and impenetrable maze."

The work was completed.

I will never cease to sing the praises of words of encouragement. But the ones mentioned here have a special place in my affections. Because some people spoke, many others got to sing!

Sunday — February 23

IN a fable, a man learns of a magical stone that can turn anything into gold. He would know it by its warmth. Unfortunately, it was somewhere on a beach full of stones.

Every day for a year he picked up stones, declared them cold and threw them into the sea. Then he picked up a warm stone. His heart jumped, his mind celebrated, and he threw the stone into the sea! Habit had conditioned his body so thoroughly that heart and mind were automatically over-ruled.

When our habits have that sort of power, let's make sure they are good ones!

Monday — February 24

A YOUNG friend told me about a computer game he was playing. In this virtual world there are characters called Exploiters. They are hackers who come into the game to mess things up for the players. They get their kicks exploiting the innocence of others, or their lack of knowledge of how the internet "world" works.

"But," he told me, "once I saw a hacker come into the world from somewhere else and make things better for the player. He helped with problems, and made their online lives better. Just once."

This serves as a reminder that exploiters are at work in the real world, too, and just the once, Jesus made everything better, despite them.

Tuesday — February 25

O N dull and wintry mornings,
When the duvet feels so warm,
And we pull our curtains back, to see
More rain and blustery storms,
Remember dark and dreary days
Like these will always end.
Just like the difficulties and
Frustrations life can send.
Tomorrow comes another day,
And look! – the sky is blue,
The sun is out, the warm spring breeze,
Blows happiness to you.

Linda Brown

Wednesday — February 26

T HE Shakespeare & Company bookshop in Paris is full of books, but some of the most important words are written on the wall.

Paraphrasing Hebrews 13, verse 2, it says, "Be not inhospitable to strangers, lest they be angels in disguise." Powerful!

I prefer a more proactive approach. Don't worry about disguises or pleasing heavenly beings. Be hospitable to people. Who knows? You might turn out to be their angel.

Fun in the sun!

IN 1913, Alexander Irvine was a successful preacher in the United States. But his life began in Antrim, Northern Ireland.

In his book "My Lady Of The Chimney Corner", he described poverty as a constant companion. His parents had married across the religious divide and were largely shunned by both communities.

They always had one thing going for them. It was what saw him through to a better life, a lesson he would never forget, and was summed up in words he wanted inscribed above his parents' grave.

What was it? The realisation that "Love is enough".

Friday — February 28

THERE was a hill I loved going down on my bike when I was a boy. One time I hit a hole in the tarmac. The hole was about six inches wide, but enough to give me a good jolt.

The next time I hurtled down that hill I remembered the hole and went straight into it, despite the rest of the road being empty and available. I hit that hole so often it buckled my front wheel.

I had become more concerned with the negative than the positive, seeing the obstacle rather than the opportunity.

It's important that we know where the problems in life are, but it's more important that we keep them in perspective. It's a much better way to enjoy the ride!

Saturday — February 29

HE had done me a great wrong in the distant past. For a while I believed I hated him. Now, here he was in front of me, counting his pennies at a shop till. And he didn't have enough.

Serves him right, I thought.

But because I strive to be better than my first instincts, I paid for his purchase.

He didn't recognise me. He was grateful. He had no idea I had just forgiven him. But I did. And my step, thereafter, was lighter because of it.

March

THESE days, it's a kitchen cupboard.
It used to be known as a pantry. Before that, the place in the kitchen for keeping the family's food was known as an ambry.

The word comes from "almery", a place to keep alms. Alms tend to be money or food given to those who have none.

The food in the almery was probably never charity. It would have been grown or worked for.

But isn't it a lovely notion that everything we need to help us thrive is given to us?

By nature; by providence. From above.

AS an experiment, or perhaps even for fun, someone suspended a large bag of salt from the ceiling, above a black floor-cloth.

They opened a hole in the bottom of the bag, then they set it swinging.

At first, it left a ragged white line on the black cloth, then it formed a rough circle. The circle thinned into an increasingly narrow oval.

Then, when it seemed there was nowhere else to go, the oval turned around ninety degrees and began expanding again. And so on.

Eventually, losing momentum, the salt drew a decreasing spiral in the middle of what was now a wonderfully intricate pattern. Other than the initial push, no-one had touched it. Gravity and momentum did the work.

My point in explaining all this? Oh, maybe nothing.

But it seems an uplifting thought to me that the world, left to its own devices, just about always tends towards the beautiful.

SOMETIMES we find we need a friend when things are dark and grey;
Someone who's there to understand and sweep our cares away.
A friend is always there when troubles pile up at one's door,
A friend will always give a helping hand – and so much more.
So many folk may need someone on whom they can depend;
Someone who helps in times of need, and YOU can be that friend.

Dennis W. Turner

Wednesday — March 4

IN 19th-century Ireland – and, no doubt, many other places – Sunday was "meat day." For people living in poverty, meat for Sunday dinner was an aspiration only sometimes achieved.

The women made a broth of whatever food was available. Then jugs of it were shared around the neighbours. Because everyone did this, each cook usually ended up with the same amount of broth.

More importantly, it meant each woman could tell, by the ingredients, who was doing well and who was struggling; who could help and who needed help.

Sharing. There's always more to it than simply sharing.

Thursday — March 5

IN a dedication to the Earl of Buchan, John Mackintosh wrote: "Happy would that nation be where every person of distinguished rank would endeavour to distinguish himself still more essentially, by being beneficial to the public, and thereby confirm our old Gaelic saying: '*bithidh meas is fearr*'." The best fruit is on the highest branch.

We might never achieve much of a "distinguished rank", but that shouldn't stop us trying to be a sweeter apple. And being beneficial to others is definitely the way to do that.

HORACE WALPOLE told a friend he was remodelling his house to create a "Beauty Room".

He had recently bought several exquisite paintings by Sir Peter Lely and thought that they deserved very special – and expensive – attention.

Walpole was an earl and his house was more of a palace. The cost of his Beauty Room would have been beyond most of our budgets. But the concept is perhaps worth considering, no matter where we live or how much money we have.

In this man-made world, where blandness is so often the theme of the day, might there be a part of your home – a room, a wall, a drawer – that you could dedicate to beauty?

I am willing to suggest that the appreciation of even a small amount of the stuff, even in the tiniest of spaces, would create a much larger Beauty Room in your heart.

At no extra cost!

Saturday — March 7

ANCIENT wisdom tells us, "Thy neighbour is thy teacher. Live with him who prays and thou prayest. Live with the singer and thou singest." Worth remembering.

If our neighbour is our teacher, then we are theirs. What neighbourly lesson would "thou" impart?

Sunday — March 8

THE Gaels of the Scottish diaspora often had no say in the matter when it came to the leaving of their homelands. So, there is, perhaps, extra poignancy in this saying of theirs, but I am sure wanderers of any nationality would understand the beauty and the emotion behind it.

"To him that farthest went away the sweetest music he ever heard was, 'Come home'."

IN the Disney animation named after him, Aladdin promises Princess Jasmine "A whole new world".

Where is this world? It's the one she already lives in – seen from his magic flying carpet. What he is actually offering is "a new fantastic point of view".

I have found that how we look at the world really does affect our experience of it. So if you are tired of the same old world and fancy something exciting and new, change your perspective: adopt a new fantastic point of view.

No flying carpet needed.

A NEW house was being built into a nearby hillside. On his regular dog-walks, Len watched the builders excavate the limestone that lay just under the topsoil.

Then he saw that same limestone put into foundations and crushed up for use in the driveways.

"It was a nice example of how God gives us everything we need," he told me once the building was complete and a family living in it. "Reshaping it into our needs can be a messy process, though."

His wife, Sue, gave him a playful nudge and added, "Just like it can be messy when God tries to reshape us for his needs."

Not to be outdone, Len kissed her cheek and said, "Of course, some of us are better raw materials to begin with."

HUSBANDRY means more than being a married man. A farmer's definition says that good husbandry is feeding the land before it gets hungry. Giving it rest before it grows weary. And weeding it before it becomes unworkable.

Is there an area of your life – be you man or woman – that could benefit from some good husbandry?

I HEARD the blackbird sing today
His anthem to the sky,
And off my thoughts went travelling,
My spirit lifted high.
The winter left behind me now
The earth once more awakes,
The trees will soon be dressed in green,
So little time it takes.
The wind will lose its winter chill
The breezes will be light,
And we'll go walking woods and fields
As days grow long and bright.
So thank you, blackbird, once again
As, one more time, I learned
Your songs have magic in their sound.
I'm glad that you returned!

Iris Hesselden

Friday — March 13

I WATCHED a young man walking towards a zebra crossing in a supermarket car park.

A car slowed down, preparing to stop for him to pass. The young man also slowed down and waved the driver on through.

Once he had actually stepped on to the crossing, another car was approaching.

He broke into a trot, clearing the road, meaning the second car didn't have to stop, either.

Slowing down and speeding up. The kind thing doesn't always have to be the same thing.

It should suit the opportunities. A philosophy I had just seen elegantly demonstrated.

What should never change, though, is the state of heart that keeps us looking for those opportunities.

KALIMA INACHUS is its fancy name, but the little creature is commonly known as the dead leaf butterfly. Why?

Well, you wouldn't guess if you were looking at the tops of its wings.

They are bright blue with splashes of yellow. But when it rests, its wings come together in the upright position and it looks exactly like – you guessed it – a dead leaf. Complete with stalk.

Given that the butterfly doesn't have the best view of its own wings and probably didn't design itself, even the most ardent unbeliever would surely have to ask, "Who paints these things?"

ONE day, I asked the Lady of the House how she had spent the afternoon.

"Panning for gold," she replied with a perfectly straight face.

I didn't ask, but she knew she had my attention.

"The old prospectors," she explained, "would sift tons of rubble in the hope of seeing an occasional precious glint of gold in their pan. I spent the afternoon listening to a woman in difficulties talking about all sorts of trivia.

"But in amongst all of that was the occasional snippet of useful information. I do believe I know how to help her."

The old prospectors didn't have coffee and cake while they were searching, like she did. And I am glad I don't have to go to any uncomfortable lengths to find gold, either.

My sweetheart has a heart full of the stuff!

IT is better to stay silent than to sing a bad song." So goes an old Scottish proverb.

Can I suggest another option, though? Wherever possible, sing a better song!

Nature's camouflage at its best.

WHERE can I find happiness?
Can you tell me, please?
Is it somehow preordained
Or floating in the breeze?
Is it unobtainable,
Just for the lucky few?
Or is it closer than I think,
Defined by what I do?
Is it banishing those selfish thoughts,
That breed such discontent,
And treating each and every day,
As if it's heaven sent?
Or giving up the yearning,
For the things that we have not,
And gratefully rejoicing,
In the life that we have got?

Linda Brown

Wednesday — March 18

IN the days when weaving was still an important cottage industry, the weavers (so I am told) used to have a saying.

"A loom that has gone awry is best handled patiently."

This meant that, if some part of the loom had come loose, it was often a preferable option to take longer to finish the job than to try to fix it and risk breaking the threads that were already woven.

A lot of good work could be lost for lack of a little patience.

The same, of course, is true with people. We can spoil a relationship by trying to "fix" someone who has "gone awry" in some way.

Whereas, with a little patience and careful handling, we might eventually guide them to a happier conclusion, and nothing need be lost.

Thursday — March 19

THE Lady of the House has a framed piece of embroidery passed down to her by Great-aunt Louisa. It's in the form of a motto and was probably meant for the women and girls of the house, but it could easily apply to any of us setting out on some new venture.

It says, "She that doesn't knot her thread will lose from the first stitch."

In other words: make sure you have your facts right; lace those boots up; check you have enough petrol; set off on the right foot, making sure everything you do has a sure foundation.

Begin by tying a metaphorical knot at the end of your thread!

Friday — March 20

A FOLK tale has an eagle and a wren arguing over who could reach the greatest heights. They decided on a competition and took to the air. After a while the eagle was feeling the frost on his feathers and a lack of oxygen.

"Ha!" He gasped. "Little wren, where are you now?"

"Higher than you are," the wren, who had hitched a lift on the eagle's back, said in his ear.

Brains will take you farther, and higher, than strength. But, of course, the proper use of strength is to lift others up.

Saturday — March 21

THE saying "*An la a chi's nach fhaic*" translates from the Gaelic as "every day – present or absent" and is usually spoken as a farewell. The expression makes no real sense on its own, but the full form begins with *beannachd leat*, which means "goodbye" or "blessings be with you."

And "goodbye" originally meant "God be with you."

God – or blessings – be with you, whether you are present or absent – that's a farewell from the heart!

Sunday — March 22

IN his work "Reminiscences Of A Highland Parish", published in the 1860s, Doctor Norman Macleod told of the passing of a minister.

The minister's wife was described as only a wife and mother.

Then Doctor Macleod added, "But who can know what service a wife and a mother is to a family, save those who have had this staff to lean on, this pillow to rest on, this sun to shine on them, this best of friends to accompany them?"

Monday — March 23

HARRY knows I am a bibliophile and I imagine he was trying to get a rise out of me when he showed me the picture.

A house-owner – perhaps in Russia or thereabouts – had repaired the pillar beside his front door with books and dollops of cement.

I looked at it, nodded approvingly (to confound him) and said, "Yet another way that books are wonderful!"

You can build the foundations of a good life on the information found between the covers of books, so why not use actual books as a physical support for your home when no bricks are readily available?

Of course, it's better if you read them first!

Tuesday — March 24

A FRIEND in need . . ."
The old saying usually ends "is a friend indeed". But many a wit and wag have come up with their own endings.

Some are intentionally humorous; some are sadly cynical.

On a trip to the Western Isles I heard a version that will for ever be my favourite.

"A friend in need is the only friend."

Contented cows.

ONE day, a man noticed a non-venomous snake being gathered up in a pile of sticks and thrown into the middle of a camp fire.

He reached in, grabbed the snake and lifted it out of danger. Of course, the snake bit him.

He dropped it and it slithered for shelter, straight back towards the fire.

He grabbed a stick from the woodpile, put it under the snake and flicked it away to safety.

His friends were amazed. He had saved the creature, been bitten in return, then saved it a second time.

"I would have beat it with that stick!" one friend said.

"I'd have let it burn," another added.

"Why?" the man asked them. "It's the snake's nature to respond to danger with violence. If I had beat it with the stick after it attacked me, I'd be doing what the snake did. I have my own nature."

As someone once said: "Shape your actions by your own character, not your enemy's."

Thursday — March 26

EVERY once in a while, perhaps by happy chance or during an excavation, a new treasure hoard will be unearthed.

It might have been buried by Saxons, Christian monks, Vikings or Romans, and each time such a thing is unearthed it gives us a clearer insight into the lives of the people back then.

Reading up on those times, I came across the word "breost-hord". It means chest-treasure and describes those items a person might hold on to the tightest and, thus, value the most.

But we might go a little deeper in search of real treasure. The things we hold in our breast, next to our hearts, are what are really important to us.

And they tell us a lot about how we live!

THE fence was built to keep farm animals in, but once there had been a path running through there, so the farmer built a sturdy stile. The fence wasn't high and the steps weren't difficult (for able-bodied folk), but people started going another way – an easier but longer way.

As I contemplated the bramble bush, flourishing where once a path had been, I thought of the good things in life: the good habits, good traditions, that require a little extra effort. If we don't keep using them, we lose them.

Often, there will be an easier way, but just as the new path is longer, so the easier way always ends up taking more from us.

The path had been a beautiful walk, but it was easily lost. I hope we take the effort to preserve what is beautiful in our lives.

Saturday — March 28

LIZ told me she had a new take on her never-ending round of housework.

Every time a shirt is ironed, a football top is folded or ballet shoes are put away, she says a little thank you, or prayer of appreciation, for the person who normally wears them.

"It doesn't make any difference in the grand scheme of things," she admitted to me with a smile, "but it does make me feel better."

Does a habit of prayer and appreciation make a difference to those being prayed for? Maybe.

Does it make any difference to the world at large? Maybe.

Does it make a difference to the person saying the prayer, or giving the thanks? Absolutely!

And does that happier, more appreciative, spiritually uplifted person then go on to make a difference in the lives of those they care for and in the well-being of the world at large?

Of course they do. It's a wonderful truth. And I am very thankful for it.

The timeless beauty of a thatched cottage.

Sunday — March 29

THE Grand Canyon has many spectacular viewpoints for tourists to enjoy the many magnificent vistas.

One of them has a sign that reads, *One minute. Don't read. Don't talk. No photos. Just look . . . and see.*

We can do that at scenes of outstanding natural beauty, in a field or in our back gardens, with places we have never seen before, or places we think we know.

What's important is that we not only look, but that we also take the time to see.

Monday — March 30

WHO hasn't admired a thatched roof, even if only in pictures? Of course, a lot of work goes into making something so elegantly beautiful. And that work must be done at the right time.

There's a saying in Ireland that "the windy day is not the day for thatch-wattles".

The thatch-wattle, generally made of willow, is the anchor that holds the thatch in place. If you haven't inserted them in placid days you will have no chance of doing so on a windy day.

In other words, be prepared.

Tuesday — March 31

OUR dear friend Mary had just recounted the time she spent four hours in a queue – and the new friends she had made there.

"You always look for the best, don't you?" I commented.

"I do," she replied happily. "And I always find it."

Before I could inject a more "realistic" note, she did it for me.

"And I know if I was to look for the worst, I would find that, too. It's all out there. I suppose the question is, in the end, what do we want to find in this life?"

I'm with Mary. I'm happy looking for the best – and always finding it.

April

ONE of Great-aunt Louisa's diaries recalls the night before her brother's voyage to America. The family gathered around the fire. Good times were recalled, apologies were offered where necessary, minds were stretched trying to imagine what America would be like.

Louisa recalls her mother saying, "Underneath and woven throughout it all was the ticking of the clock and the thought that we might never see him again. Each minute seemed made of gold."

They did see him again. He did rather well for himself out there!

But the idea of minutes being like gold has stayed with me. Some seem desperately important; others are deliberately squandered. But none will come again, so each ought to be considered precious.

It's up to us to make as many of them as we can "golden".

A GARDENER, writing in 1947, suggested that April should be approached with caution.

Many of the plants in our gardens, he said, were still feeling the effects of a harsh winter. Some might look beyond saving. We should be tender. We should give them time. We should be prepared for delightful surprises later in the year, when they find enough strength to blossom again.

The advice fits my own gardening experience, and it also fits my experience of those who have gone through their own personal "winter". Patience, in relationships as with gardening, is always a virtue. Difficult times may take longer for some to recover from than others.

May we not be too quick to "prune back" or "uproot". May we enjoy those delightful late blooms when they arrive!

Friday — April 3

A MAN of the church once compared jobs with a ploughman. "I keep both hands to my work," he said. "I keep my eyes fixed on where I want to go, and I plough as straight a furrow as I possibly can. Thus far, I think I have done a pretty good job. There have been very few things that have tilted my plough this way or that."

Nodding in general agreement, the ploughman thought the churchman could benefit from one more thing – a little humility.

"Sure, and any man can plough a straight furrow if it's shallow," he said. "But the rocks and roots that really test your skill lie deeper than the surface. Tell me again when you can plough deep and straight."

Saturday — April 4

IT is one of the best descriptions of a person I have ever heard.

Our dear friend Mary, whose family came from a farming background, described her great-grandmother thus: "She lived a potato-sack life", meaning her clothes were often patched with, or even made from, potato sacks, "but she herself was fine linen."

Never let your circumstances define you. Be fine linen on the inside, no matter what you wear on the outside.

Sunday — April 5

THANK you for the laughter
Of small children as they pass,
Thank you for the heavenly smell
Of freshly new cut grass.
Thank you for the simple pleasures
Tasted every minute,
In this glorious world of ours
That has such wonder in it.

Linda Brown

Monday — April 6

THE artist Jorge Mendez Blake built a wall 13 feet high and 75 feet long. Under two bricks in the bottom row, he placed a book. This lifted them somewhat. Those two bricks lifted three in the next row. Those three lifted four, and so on.

By the last row, dozens of bricks had been shifted out of place, disturbing what might otherwise have been a uniform barrier.

The end effect was out of all proportion to the size of the book. This is how books make a difference in our societies. There's a knock-on effect; a spreading outwards of the original idea.

It is also how kind words make a difference in lives.

Tuesday — April 7

ONE of Edinburgh's less famous "attractions" is the set of stone steps joining the New Town to the Royal Mile. For many of the city's visitors arriving at Waverley Station, the steps are an unexpected exertion, but one mum had a different take.

I overheard her telling her complaining children, "You can look at each step as something in your way to complain about, or as an opportunity to stand taller and see further. You decide!"

Indeed. We decide!

Wednesday — April 8

THERE is a Russian story about a rouble that couldn't be spent. It's a simple tale. Every time someone bought something with this particular rouble, their change would include the same coin they made the purchase with. No matter who spent it, it always returned to them.

That mythical rouble is sometimes taken as a metaphor for love, the point being that if you give love, you get love in return. I'd like to agree with it. It's a lovely idea.

But in my experience it's not true! Rather, I have found that if you give one "rouble" worth of love, you will, one way or another, get two in return. Or three. Or four. Or ten!

Thursday — April 9

SOPHOCLES, the Greek playwright, wrote, "One must wait until the evening to see how splendid the day has been."

It is a golden time, isn't it? Of course, the day might not always seem splendid. In which case, look for the lessons it offered. They will provide a solid foundation for a splendid tomorrow.

Friday — April 10

BOOKS have been my passion since I was old enough to spend my pocket money on them. But I have loved stories longer!

The ones I love best are told by the people who experienced them, and teach me of worlds I haven't known.

In putting together a collection of tales told by farming folk in the 1800s, William Littlejohn talked about the power stories have to rest and soothe our soul. In 1929, he wrote, "Our present day is made up of rush, bustle, and feverish excitement!"

What he would have made of the year 2020 we can only wonder! Thankfully, where friends and companions gather together, we still have stories to share for the good they do.

I believe – as Mr Littlejohn did – that stories are an essential part of who we are. They do us more good than we ever could imagine.

Saturday — April 11

DID you ever feel, in some way, incomplete? I think many of us have felt that way at one time or another.

Some fill that space very effectively with God or love. Others fill it differently.

We often think of that feeling as a negative thing, but perhaps it is important to have that lack, so that we might fill it, and hopefully fill it well.

These were my thoughts as I watched a potter make a clay bowl on her throwing wheel.

"The bowl is made of clay," she told us, "but it is the empty space inside it that makes it of any use at all."

Sunday — April 12

THE new believer wandered over to a baptism being conducted on the beach.

Chatting to one of the group gathered there, he mentioned that faith was a relatively new experience for him.

"Ah, yes," the older, and doubtlessly more experienced, man said. "You still have that look about you."

That look? Joy? Peace? Happiness?

"May it never fade."

At this time of rebirth, let our faith be reborn, fresh and vibrant, each new God-given morning.

Monday — April 13

MY friend Ken is a pastor, so when he posted "Evening Prayers" on social media, I expected something . . . well, churchy!

What I found was a video taken from the beach at Cleveleys in Lancashire. The setting sun painted the sky in oranges and reds, the waves rolled on to the beach, and Mary's Shell – a large metal sculpture – was half submerged in the sea.

Ken said not a word. His prayer, it seemed, was a silent appreciation of the beauty of it all. I watched his video more than once, and felt my soul being soothed each time.

Tuesday — April 14

STORMY wind, you woke me, you stirred me from my rest,
Through sleep I heard you singing within the chimney breast.
I rose, and through my window, I saw a rain-swept sky,
The trees alive and dancing, the clouds all streaming by.

Wild wind, for ever whirling, you chase across the globe,
No corner left unheeded, no place you cannot probe.
Oh, how I long to travel, within your wings safe-curled,
To race, in endless freedom, across the wide blue world.

Maggie Ingall

HELEN tells me that when her daughter was two years old, she read a "Mummies And Babies" book to her. It was a picture book with cows and calves, sheep and lambs, cats and kittens and so on.

After a moment's thought, her daughter asked, "Mum, who was God's mummy?"

The little girl grew up to be a mummy, and her four-year-old daughter was in the car seat behind Helen recently when she went into a reverie. Then she asked, "Granny Helen, was there ever a time before the world was builded?"

"I could use this as a chance to say how smart my little ones are," Helen told me. "But I would rather encourage people to listen to children more. They go a lot deeper than many adults!"

How could I disagree?

Thursday — April 16

GREAT-AUNT LOUISA, in one of her diaries, recalled a neighbour being very frustrated.

The local iron-worker who promised to repair a boot scraper; a man hired to paint the hallway; a temporary house-maid hired to cover the regular maid's holidays – each had added to his workload rather than reduced it.

"Having had enough for one day," he told her, "I planted some mustard and cress and retired at nine p.m."

The mustard and cress seemed an odd inclusion in his litany of woes, but Louisa explained.

"The people we encounter in any ordinary day doubtlessly have their own concerns and priorities, of which we often know little. Often, and usually without intending to, they might frustrate another's desires, bringing their work to naught.

"Nature and God, on the other hand, will always take your best effort and unselfishly make more of it. The few minutes he spent planting those seeds would, I am sure, have been a great reassurance to him."

A beautiful sunset is one of nature's wonders.

STACEY has a picture of herself at the far end of Portencross pier in Ayrshire. The photographer stood behind her, catching her silhouette against a choppy sea and the setting sun.

"It's a lovely picture," she told me, "but I don't keep it because it's beautiful. The pier is ramshackle, and halfway along there's a big hole. The thought of falling through it stopped me in my tracks, even though there was plenty of space to walk either side of it.

"I just could not envisage myself getting past it. But where I am standing in the photo is a good twenty yards further on. It's my permanent reminder that most of the things we think will stop us can be walked around – and left behind."

Saturday — April 18

A MAN and his son were remembering a farmer who had died. The son remembered the farmer had three beautiful, well brought up and kind daughters.

His father remembered when the son had come home covered in sour milk for getting too close to one of the daughters.

The mother remonstrated with her husband, saying the son had remembered three good things about the farmer, while he had remembered only a single bad thing.

How often does it happen that we let one negative thing "sour" us to all the positive?

Sunday — April 19

THERE are three words for love used in the Bible. They are "agape", which means loving everyone; "philea", describing a deep affection; and "eros", which refers to passion.

Other words describe other types of love, but I have to agree with the American theologian Reinhold Niebuhr, who suggested that one word described love's final form. What was that word? The one Niebuhr thought would save us all? Jesus spoke of it on the cross.

It is forgiveness.

Monday — April 20

TAKE a little time each day,
However busy you might be.
Look around at earth and sky,
The beauty of each plant and tree.
Take a little time at night;
See the first bright star on high,
As the clouds all disappear,
Watch the moon sail through the sky.
Take a moment now and then,
Whatever tasks you need to do:
Relax, be happy, share a smile,
Take a little time for you!

Iris Hesselden

Tuesday — April 21

THE house faced out towards the beach. When I saw the sign in the window I naturally assumed it was advertising vacant rooms for holiday-makers. But no.

Instead, it read *This Is Our Happy Place*. That brought my widest smile of the day.

A family home has to be so many things: a shelter from the world, an investment for the future, a place to raise children. But making your home your happy place should always be a priority.

Wednesday — April 22

She stood on the shore on a blustery day. She wrote these words in the sand with a stick: "LIFE IS GOOD".

Trying to make sure my enthusiastic canine companion didn't jump over her work, I agreed, and we spent a few minutes chatting.

As I walked away, a wave splashed my shoe and I said, "You know the tide will wipe that out, don't you?"

"Aye," she replied, "and sometimes the feeling gets washed away as well. But I know two other things. I know the tide always turns and I know I will write those words again."

HAVE you heard of "Imposter Syndrome"?
It is the notion that, whatever you are doing, people will soon discover that you are only pretending to be good at it; and that you are actually a fake, while everyone else out there is the real deal.

Few people talk about it. But when they do, others often respond, "Really? I thought I was the only one!"

The dramatist W.S. Gilbert might have used the term to describe himself, if he'd known it.

As one half of Gilbert and Sullivan, he was undoubtedly a literary and theatrical genius, but he wrote, "You have no idea what a poor opinion I have of myself, and how little I deserve it."

If, like Gilbert, you think yourself an imposter – someone who is making it up as they go along – and that causes you to have a poor opinion of yourself, then take it from me: you don't deserve it, either.

We are all making our lives up as we go along. Really!

THE Highland saying goes, "A house with a closed door can't be kept." But why?

Remembering the tradition of Highland hospitality, I understood better.

The closed door shuts out neighbours as well as those in need. Which is fine when the household is doing well, but at some point we all need a neighbour's assistance.

The man or woman who looked to us for help (and didn't find it) might have had an upturn in their fortunes and be disinclined to share with us.

Thus, the house with a closed door does well for a time. Then it is lost.

The same applies when we try to live our lives with closed hearts.

May we, for the whole world's sake, learn to live with welcoming hearts and hospitable homes.

FOR too long, in my opinion, the gloomier sort have got away with claiming the expression "I'm being realistic" as their own.

Writing in 1947 about realism in literature, Sir John Squire discussed two favourite authors. He said, "It is true that their temperament gave their work a comic bias, as the temperaments of most of the other 'realists' gave theirs a gloomy bias."

When there are different views of the world, surely no-one has any claim to holding the definitive one. Each is as valid to the person experiencing it as any other.

If you will indulge me that far, then you will surely forgive me (and hopefully smile) when, after telling of people being better than they might be, and the world being more wonderful than we might imagine, I end by saying, "I'm only being realistic!"

Sunday — April 26

AROUND the turn of the twentieth century there was, in print, a gardening handbook called "Flowers That Do Not Disappoint". It contained the warning that every flower would disappoint if it was planted carelessly, and not tended regularly.

Good advice for gardeners, but also for those in new romantic relationships, people striking up friendships and expectant parents.

In fact, for everyone who would like a relationship, of whatever kind, to blossom.

Monday — April 27

IN the movie "Wind River", one character confesses to another, "I get so mad, I want to fight the whole world. You know what that feels like?"

His friend replies, "I do. But I decided to fight the feeling instead . . . because I figured the world would win."

It reminded me of the old saying, "He who conquers others is strong; he who conquers himself is mighty!" And smart!

Our most important battles are usually fought in our heart.

Tuesday — April 28

DO you ever feel life is unfair, or that more than your fair share of trouble is piled on your shoulders?

Life is unfairly difficult for some, but for most of us the weight lies in our imagination and our fears rather than in reality. It has always been thus, but it need not always be so.

Solon, a statesman of ancient Athens, wrote, "If all our misfortunes were laid in one common heap, whence every one must take an equal portion, most people would be content to take their own and depart."

Wednesday — April 29

SOME children were shown a photo of the galaxy taken by the Hubble telescope. Some of them saw pretty stars; one thought they could see a prancing unicorn; another thought they could make out a baby's face.

The French novelist Marcel Proust said, "The universe is true for us all, and dissimilar to each of us."

Thursday — April 30

MINISTERS, philosophers and other learned people have tried for centuries to express what death must be like. It's a question that will occur to most of us.

What is perhaps my favourite description did not come from a theologian, or from some ancient scripture.

It came from the writer of an episode of the popular TV programme "The Waltons".

In "The Boy From The CCC", a tough city kid named Gino comes to live with the family and, of course, there is trouble. But when Elizabeth Walton's pet raccoon dies and she is distraught, Gino tries to comfort her.

When she asks what death is, Gino replies, "I think it's just closing your eyes, and instead of seeing darkness you see the light."

May it be so.

May

HIS love is like a gentle breeze,
That brushes my cheek and travels with ease.
His love is like the open sea
So wide and deep and flowing free.
His love is like the prettiest flower
That brings such joy in a dismal hour,
His love is like the sun's warm rays,
Brightening even the saddest of days.
His love is like a crystal stream
That sparkles with the sunshine's gleam.
His love is like a warm embrace
Making our troubles fade without trace.
He loves us with a love so true
That we can't help but love him, too.

Amanda-Jayne Lanceley

THE path was worn bare in the middle by a multitude of horses' hooves over years of use.

To either side were ruts made by the wheels of the carts the horses pulled.

In the space between the wheel ruts and the horses' path, the writer and philosopher Henry David Thoreau saw a flower grow, blossom and live out its natural span, unperturbed by all that went on to either side of it.

Now, we are not flowers and we cannot ignore the rest of the world, but neither should we let the fear of this and that prevent us from blossoming where we are.

Sunday — May 3

WHEN I met Harry, he was walking into town. He explained that he had been to lunch with friends at a particular café and now he was going shopping.

I was confused. He was actually heading in the direction of the café he claimed to have just come from.

I challenged this and he admitted he'd seen a man, carrying two heavy bags, walking with a stick and shaking from the exertion. So Harry had walked with him, past the shop he had intended visiting, all the way to the man's home. Now he was on his way back.

He ended by adding, "It wasn't out of the way."

"It was a hundred and eighty degrees and a mile out of your way!" I protested.

"Oh, sure." He laughed with a twinkle in his eye that suggested he had caught me out. "I was out of my way. But today I have been practising walking with God. And it wasn't out of his way at all."

Monday — May 4

IN the days when circuses still had elephants, the animal-wrangler would tie a rope around the baby elephant's foot.

He would fasten the other end to a stake driven into the ground, and this would be enough to prevent it wandering off.

They did this often enough that, even when the elephant was bigger and could easily pull the stake out of the ground, it didn't. Why not? Because its younger self couldn't.

All too often people stay wedded to fears, limitations or beliefs that were formed when they were too young to know any better. Those notions may have been relevant and important in times gone by, but no longer.

Never be stopped by something you could easily free yourself from, if only you believed you could!

Tug at that rope every once in a while. And see if it still holds you back.

Looking out to sea.

Cliffs at Marwick Head, Orkney Isles.

Tuesday — May 5

IF, when we were young, we could see the trials that awaited us, we might never want to grow older.

Likewise, the dollop of clay might be happy being a dollop and fear the spinning wheel that helps turn it into a fine bowl.

Charles Dickens meant something similar when, in "Great Expectations", he wrote, "I have been bent and broken, but – I hope – into a better shape."

When facing those trials, don't fear. Have your own great expectations instead.

Wednesday — May 6

HOW would you like to be a genius?
Wolfgang Amadeus Mozart – a musical genius if ever there was one – credited his abilities less to something he was born with, and more to his passion for music.

"Neither a lofty degree of intelligence nor imagination nor both together, go to the making of genius," he is said to have explained. "Love, love, love, that is the soul of genius."

Now, some may argue with me when I suggest people might achieve genius status if they love what it is they do enough, but, I wonder, would they argue with Mozart?

Thursday — May 7

WE stood on the cliff top, on the west side of Hoy, one of the Orkney Isles.

I say "stood", but we were leaning into the wind coming in off the sea.

Chae, in an attempt at positivity, shouted over to me.

"The wind never blew that didn't fill someone's sail!"

Aye, I thought (to save my words being blown away), there is much good in this world that we ignore, or disparage, simply because it doesn't work for us at that time. But it will still be good!

HAVE you ever heard the expression "A man's smile is not his own"?

It doesn't signify the smile is fake. It means that a man or woman might be wearing the smile, but it partly belongs to the person who inspired it.

Here's to the smilers – and the people who gave them something to smile about!

Saturday — May 9

PHIL works with children. Over the years this has included some rather difficult times and also some heart-breaking occasions, but, overall, he finds it uplifting and wouldn't want to do anything else.

Perhaps I was being a little pretentious when I tried to sum up his feelings with this quote from Fyodor Dostoevsky – "The soul is healed by being with children."

"Hmm," was Phil's considered response. "If by 'healed' you mean broken into bits, then glued and taped back together into a wonderful new shape before being painted bright colours and covered in sparkles, then yeah."

How wonderful!

Sunday — May 10

SOMEONE to listen,
Someone to cheer,
Somewhere, a shoulder
When shedding a tear.
Somewhere the kindness
To help us in need:
Gems to be treasured,
Of friendship, indeed!

Elizabeth Gozney

Monday — May 11

THE TV series "The Waltons" told of a family living in the mountains of Virginia. One of the buildings used as their home is actually in the Warner Brothers lot in California. It is surrounded by trees, just like in the programme, but those trees are surrounded by busy roads and bustling film studios.

Now, we can look at that in two ways. If we stood in those trees and looked out, we might easily be convinced that everything is fake. If we stood in those trees and looked in, we might easily believe that peace and tranquillity can be found anywhere.

Tuesday — May 12

G.K. CHESTERTON had a way of taking everyday thoughts and raising them – or perhaps restoring them – to a higher level.

"You say grace before meals. All right. But I say grace before the play and the opera, and grace before the concert and pantomime, and grace before I open a book, and grace before sketching, painting, swimming, fencing, boxing, walking, playing, dancing; and grace before I dip the pen in the ink."

In all things, seek guidance and give thanks!

Wednesday — May 13

STACEY showed me a text message on her phone. The part I saw began with her thanking her dad for something. It ended with the words, *You're the best!*

She scrolled down a little and I saw her father's reply.

It's been one of my life's greatest missions to be the best dad you've ever had.

Dad! her next response read. *You're the only dad I've ever had!*

Then there was a *Yeah* followed by several smiley faces and the words *But I'm not going to let that fact stop me trying.*

You decide what your goals are in this life. And don't let the facts stop you achieving them.

Sunset glory over Virginia mountains.

James River, Virginia, USA.

Thursday — May 14

IT was only a wee summer shower," she told Mary and me. "And he had been in the house all morning, so I told him he could still go out to play if he wanted to. And for good measure I told him what our grannies always told us: 'You're neither sugar nor salt, and you'll not melt'."

"I remember that saying," Mary said as we walked away. "And it's a good one. But I know that wee boy. He is quite sweet. A salt-of-the-earth sort, actually."

There are few things so complete in their wisdom that our dear friend can't add something to them!

Friday — May 15

AT first glance, the old saying "Friends can't be helped without a bother" might seem to suggest that helping people is a bother.

It also suggests that a friend, finding themselves in a spot of bother, is the one who might best be helped. In other words, it's someone's misfortune that gives others the opportunity to be a good friend.

Without that, we might all roll along our separate ways. So "bother", difficult though it might be, is not always such a bad thing.

Saturday — May 16

APPARENTLY – although I have never been there – there is a town in Sri Lanka called Naa mi n'yala, which means "the King knows about me".

There have been many kings, emperors and governors throughout Sri Lanka's long history, so which king the name refers to is in some doubt. Whoever he was, his fame probably never spread far beyond the island.

But isn't it a comfort to know that, wherever you might be in the world, there is a King who not only knows about you, but also loves you?

70

RYAN went white-water rafting for the first time recently. "We sat on the sides of the inflatable raft," he told me. "We each had a paddle in our hands and we steadied ourselves by tucking a foot into the crease between the sides and the bottom of the boat."

Amazingly, only one of the novice paddlers fell out the boat. That young man fell into the river eight times in ten minutes.

Once, he was hauled into the boat by his buoyancy aid, and fell right out the other side!

"Why?" I asked Ryan. "What was different about him?"

"He was the only non-swimmer in the group," Ryan explained. "He'd been certain he would end up in the water before we started. I guess his fear made itself come true."

What we believe has power!

Monday — May 18

SIR RICHARD MAITLAND, who lived all the way back in the 16th century, was an eminent judge who went blind at the age of sixty-five.

Thinking he could no longer practise law, and not yet ready to retire from a productive life, he turned to the study of – of all things – literature.

He then went on to make something of a name for himself as a poet.

Now, the good judge may have needed someone to write his poems down, and he probably never saw one of them in print, but not being able to see the end result of his endeavours did not stop him adding to the world's store of beauty.

Nor should it stop us.

Too often people hesitate to help because they can't see how it will all work out in the end.

Don't let that concern you. If you have beauty, kindness or even poetry to give, then set it free in the world.

It will take care of itself from there.

Tuesday — May 19

HOW many times have I heard people say, "It's a small world", then recount stories of meeting people from home in far-flung places, or discovering they were actually related to the most unexpected people, or finding a friend in common?

So often that I am afraid I have grown a little tired of it.

Here's a thought. Why don't we thank the old phrase for its service and then retire it? And what would we replace "It's a small world" with?

How about "It's a big family"?

Wednesday — May 20

IN the 1800s, Fritz Reuter, a German novelist, penned a most beautiful description of life, its troubles and its ideal condition. I thought it deserved to be shared here and I hope you do as well.

"No-one's life," he wrote, "flows on such an even course that it does not sometimes come up against a dam and whirl round and round, or somebody throws a stone into the clear water. Something happens to everyone, and he must take care that the water stays clear and that heaven and earth are reflected in it."

Thursday — May 21

THE book "Passages From The Life Of A Daughter At Home", written by Sarah Stephen and published in the mid-1800s, is full of charming notions.

In it, the author describes the happiness of children as they go forth with so much freedom and joy of heart to every object of delight.

To this I say, the joy of life is not a gift like other gifts, prone to breaking or wearing out.

You will see it in the eyes of the old almost as often as in the eyes of the young. If you find you have misplaced yours, then by all means reclaim it! It will have been waiting for you to do so.

One drop of water
spreads ripples.

No sunbeams pierced the sky today,
We huddled in the rain;
Relentless storms kept pressing in
To soak us once again.

Now, as day gives way to night,
Clouds billow just the same,
But out upon their distant edge
There glows a rim of flame

Reminding us that when life's storms
Around us crash and roar,
There, beyond the darkest cloud,
The spirit yet can soar

And see the glory still to come,
A future yet unknown;
God's promise of a brighter day
When stormy times have flown.

Marion Cleworth

DID you ever wish you were perfect? Complete? If you ever look at a moth's wing under a microscope, you might get a surprise. You see, it isn't perfect. It isn't complete. It's full of holes.

But those holes make the wings flexible and light. Air tries to pass through the holes, but causes turbulence that blocks them.

Those "imperfections" actually make the moth's wings much more efficient.

Perhaps our imperfections can also be a blessing for us. But in what way?

Well, having failings to overcome – and overcoming them – can only make us better people.

J.P. GREAVES was an unusual man. Living in England in the 18th and 19th centuries, he devised his own method of schooling, advocated vegetarianism, sought to improve the lot of agricultural workers and formed a philosophical society. His friends described him as "unique and absolutely indefinable".

Perhaps I may have disagreed with him on a point or two if we had been able to converse, but I couldn't possibly disagree with the main thrust of his belief system, which was that there is a divine source of love within each of us. And the best way to spend a life is to "pour out in full and copious streams the love and goodness we bear to all of those around us".

Monday — May 25

THERE'S a Spanish saying that translates as, "It takes two to make a quarrel, but one to end it."

We know that, but are still often reluctant to be that one.

From somewhere we have picked up the idea that the one who keeps the peace is the loser, while the one who stays stubborn is the winner.

Any donkey can be stubborn. The peace-makers – they are few and far between. They save the world a lot of strife and hurt.

I hear God calls them blessed. And I call them blessings.

Be the one.

Tuesday — May 26

DAVID is an activities co-ordinator for school children. He was about to step in and help an eight-year-old boy who "couldn't do" something, when another boy said, "What you mean is, you can't do it yet. Here, let's try again."

Eight, or eighty: there's always time to learn how to do something you couldn't before!

Wednesday — May 27

BESIDE the cathedral in Salzburg is a statue of a robed and seated man.

It is called Die Pieta and is taken by many to represent Christ weeping for the world. It certainly conveys a powerful feeling of sorrow.

But the statue itself wasn't what caught my attention. His hands and the hem of his robe seemed a little more polished than the rest of the rough, dull surface.

Why, I wondered.

My only guess is that a number of people have felt the urge to reach out and touch – and give comfort to – this sad "man". In doing so, they have caused those parts of him to shine a little brighter.

If we can do that for a statue . . .

Thursday — May 28

MY friend Harry was visiting the town recently. He was wandering in the chapel grounds, when the six o'clock bell rang.

Seeing someone he hoped was from the church, he asked the significance of the sound at that particular hour, and was told it was the Angelus bell.

"It refers to the time that Gabriel took God's message to Mary," the man explained to him. "And it reminds us to listen out for God talking to us."

"I had half a mind to buy myself a little bell and carry it everywhere with me, ringing it every now and then. But that would look weird!" Harry said when he was telling me afterwards about this encounter.

We both laughed at his words, but somehow I sensed that we both understood the underlying importance of what he was saying.

Always listen out for God – whatever time it might be.

TWO young men of our acquaintance passed their driving tests at the same time.

After a year of being on the road, one was disenchanted with his fellow drivers. The majority, he decided, were unhelpful and rude.

The other was regularly delighted by the little courtesies he saw between fellow travellers.

They both live in the same area. So what made the difference?

I wouldn't like to say, for I count them both as friends. But you might see something there that might be helpful on your journey.

WHEN Thomas Arnold, the 19th-century historian and headmaster of Rugby School, talked about his sister overcoming selfishness, he did not mean to suggest she was selfish as we might think it.

He meant she gave ever-decreasing thought to her own desires and ever-increasing thought to the happiness of others.

As a result, despite being in poor health she enjoyed "everything lovely, graceful, beautiful, high-minded, whether in God's work or man's, with the keenest relish" and brought not a cloud to "mar the beauty of Christ's spirit's glorious work".

HERE once more, stretched out before us,
Awaits another morning chorus;
Thrush and blackbird will combine
To sing their notes, pure and divine,
As sparrows twitter and martins dart,
(What a way for a day to start).
Then, suddenly, a little lark rises,
Another one of those surprises,
Then, to complete her masterclass,
Nature puts a sheen on grass.

Brian H. Gent

June

A FRIEND of mine is an author. She's not famous, but she keeps on doing what makes her heart sing.

She recently told me about her positive comments file. Actually, it's an old milk jug she keeps on her writing desk.

Whenever someone sends her an encouraging message, or says something nice about her work, she prints it off, folds it up, and drops it in the file.

Then, if she gets a bad review or an unkind comment (which she never prints off), she can read through the positive comments and remind herself that she actually can write.

A positive comments file! Wouldn't that be a wonderful thing to start? Better still, send someone a comment worth starting their own file for!

IF only I had skills to paint
This world in all its sweet delight,
Why, even toiling day and night
I could not work without constraint.
My efforts fail, my sighs be plaint,
For how to capture scent or light?
Or sun, or song, or star-filled night?
Oh, no! The bravest heart would faint.
Yet though my brushes idle stay,
My thankful gaze will still abide
On every joy that's new unfurled,
On each and every lovely day.
Not canvas-bound, but deep inside,
I'll hold and keep this wondrous world.

Maggie Ingall

Wednesday — June 3

WE cannot control how other people see us.
The poet Dame Edith Sitwell was largely unimpressed by the writing of the acclaimed novelist Virginia Woolf. But she did tell a friend she thought Woolf was a beautiful knitter!

Don't despair if others don't appreciate the attributes you would most have them notice. They may be busy admiring an aspect of you that you had never even considered.

Thursday — June 4

THROUGHOUT the history of humanity, one topic has engaged writers, artists and each of us more than any other. How can it be that we still find new things to say, write and sing about love?

Perhaps the 17th-century Prince de Marcillac had the answer, even if he didn't completely understand it.

"It is difficult to define love; all we can say is, that in the soul it is a desire to rule, in the mind it is a sympathy, and in the body it is a hidden and delicate wish to possess what we love – plus many mysteries."

We can take or leave his opinions of the effects of love on the soul, the mind and the body, while agreeing that the best answer lies in his afterthought: "plus many mysteries."

Friday — June 5

AN old Gaelic saying suggests of a man that "He has no fault at all, except that of Fingal."

Fingal, in the epic sagas of days gone by, was a hero. There is even a cave on the Isle of Staffa named after him. But he was shorter than all those who accompanied him.

How short? Eight feet tall. But his companions were even taller.

Like so many things we see as faults and difficulties these days, Fingal's fault was relative; a problem only from a certain point of view.

Standing alone, accepted for what it is, it is actually no fault at all.

May we never lose the art of conversation.

A MAN I know describes himself as a "conversation starter" on social media.

Actually, and I'm sure he would smile at me saying this, he's more of a "pot stirrer". He does seem to enjoy shaking things up.

But good conversations? They take on a life of their own. One that starts about the weather can end up in shared secrets, eased pains, help offered or a new feeling that someone cares.

Conversations, in the right hands, can be powerful forces for good. Each one is just so full of possibilities.

Why not start a new one – perhaps with someone you haven't spoken to before – today?

IN "The God of All Comfort" Hannah Whitall Smith tells of a family who move to a town where they know no-one.

After his first afternoon of play their young son tells his mother he has met a little girl, and she is so nice he never wants to move home again.

Mother asks the girl's name and he replies, "Jesus."

"Surely not!" Mother says, to which he replies, "Well, she was so lovely I did not know what else she could be called but Jesus!"

May we never be too old to learn from little children.

IN Robert Browning's poem "Paracelsus", the medical student who will become the great doctor of the title addresses his friend, Festus, explaining his desire to leave home and better himself

"There are two points in the adventure of the diver," he says. "One – when, a beggar, he prepares to plunge. One – when, a prince, he rises with his pearl."

For a life to be experienced to the full, it should surely contain both points!

Tuesday — June 9

IT was overheard advice from a seasoned runner to an enthusiastic young beginner.

"The most difficult bit isn't the first half-mile. And it's not the last hundred yards. The race is won or lost over six inches. That's the six inches between your ears, where you either believe you can or you can't do it."

It applies to every aspect of the race of life!

Wednesday — June 10

I STOOD perfectly still in a wildflower meadow. Out loud, I said, "Give me a sign. Show me a miracle."

You will never guess what happened next!

Nothing.

As I waited, I listened. I looked closer. I breathed in and out.

Then I realised it was all a sign. And every bit of it – myself included – was a miracle!

Thursday — June 11

THE novelist John Buchan once remarked on the relationship between Scottish common folk and their working dogs, their horses and so on.

Having found frequent respectful references to various creatures in verse and song, he suggested the warmth and intimacy which attends the subject in Scots poetry comes largely from the richness of the Scots language in kindly diminutives.

Kindly diminutives. Soft words showing maternal or paternal affection.

A people can be kind without having kind words in its language. But if they are unkind, such words are unlikely to ever appear.

But language and national characteristics are topics too big to discuss here. Instead, we might each tackle a smaller subject – making sure our own speech has as many "kindly diminutives" in it as we can manage.

Friday — June 12

THREE years after World War II, when we still had rationing, the country was working hard to rebuild and the situation for many people often seemed bleak.

Vita Sackville West wrote, "Agreeable incidents do continue to occur from time to time . . . and there still seem to be days when things marvellously go right instead of wrong, rarities to be recorded before they can be forgotten."

She then went on to describe the delights of a 10-mile drive through "orchard country" in Kent.

But what went right in her day is not the point I am making here.

I am encouraging you, if I may, to do as Mrs Sackville-West did and record those days when things go unexpectedly right, in the hope that you will gather enough of them to dispute her description of them as rarities.

The good days are, thankfully, more common than most people think.

Saturday — June 13

THIS particular part of the country park was a short-cut from the car park to the swing park. Children darted between the trees in their hurry to have fun. Parents followed with dogs and picnics.

The end result is some soil erosion, and I heard someone complain as he tripped over an exposed tree root. Many roots criss-cross that unofficial path, showing they were never really all that deep beneath the ground.

There are several different types of tree around that spot, and the curious thing is that the roots go under and above each other. As they grow, they form an ever-strengthening net. A safety net, if you like.

Should a storm come along, it would struggle to blow one tree over because the roots of all the others would be helping hold it upright.

I always think of community when I pass that way, where everyone is supported by everyone else.

Sunday — June 14

POLITICAL issues have a disappointing habit of causing division, with people on each side refusing to see any good in the other.

But there is often good to be found in both sides. And those good points might easily outweigh the details that separate."

Sir William Bragg, who won the Nobel Prize for Physics in 1915, was talking about faith and science opposing each other, but the same principle might just as well be applied to any set of opposing forces, should they choose to work together.

Christianity and science are opposed, was his belief, but only in the same sense as a thumb and forefinger are opposed.

Between them, one can grasp anything.

Monday — June 15

HAVE you ever heard the sound of hostas being eaten by snails? A strange question, I do realise. But my neighbour, whose potted plants were allegedly feeding the local snail population, informed me that it sounds exactly like raindrops popping as they hit the ground.

There is much to be said, and things to be learned, from sitting in silence in your garden of an evening.

I do recommend it!

Tuesday — June 16

OH, it was miserable," my young friend insisted. "It seemed like it would never end. It was cold, wet, there was no colour, no beauty.

"And then we stepped out of the cloud. More than that – we stepped out of and above the cloud that had wrapped itself around the hillside. We could see the summit and the sun shone so brightly. We saw what people so rarely see: the top of the clouds beneath us!"

Stuck in a "cloud"? Don't give up. Keep rising!

On top of the world.

Mount Everest, Nepal.

THE Lady of the House has been playing peacemaker between two good friends who have fallen out.

When she came home after the latest attempt, I noticed tears on her cheeks.

"Oh, my darling," I said. "I understand. It's frustrating enough to make anyone cry."

"I'm not crying," she replied with a brave laugh. "I've decided my soul needs to grow a little bigger to deal with this. So I'm watering it."

Having no words to respond, I hugged her, and wondered if my own soul could do with a little more watering.

Thursday — June 18

HELEN was on holiday in Rome recently. As her photo collection showed, Rome is not short of sights to see.

Her favourite place was, without a doubt, the Colosseum.

I asked her what she liked about it. She thought long and hard, then the perfect explanation occurred to her.

"It is proof," she said, "that you can be old and you can be broken, but you can still be magnificent!"

Friday — June 19

I HAVE said many times that we never really get to know all the good unleashed in the world by a single kind act. But Dr David Hamilton tried to figure it out.

In a project called the 3-Degree Ripple Rule, he showed how someone on the receiving end of a kind act will generally pass that good feeling on to others. And they will pass it on to yet another group.

He estimated – conservatively – that for each act of kindness done to an individual, sixteen people will be positively affected.

How many people would you like to cheer up today?

Saturday — June 20

WALKING through the park, I was thinking how lovely it all was. Then I started to gain on another walker. He had a carrier bag and I noticed he stopped every so often to pick things up.

I realised that, while it surely wasn't his primary purpose, in picking up the litter he found he was actually making my walk a prettier one.

The park has been around a long time. Others planted the saplings that became the trees in whose shade I walked. Still others had built the bridge I rested on to watch the river flow.

Generations of gardeners had maintained the park. All so I (and others) might enjoy it.

My friend with the bag of litter brought home to me how much we owe those who went before us, in so many aspects of life.

What can we do to thank them? Nothing, but do likewise for those who will walk the path after us.

Sunday — June 21

AS I waited in line to pay for my lunch, I realised the scruffily dressed man next to me was singing quietly to himself.

"You're singing," I said. "Are you having a good day?"

He gave the question serious consideration. "No. I'm actually having a pretty bad day," he said. "But isn't that the best time to sing?"

I paid for his lunch – and the lesson. Then I left the coffee shop humming my new friend's tune.

Monday — June 22

ONE woman was describing an absent friend to another woman, and I happened to overhear one of the loveliest compliments ever. We could also take it as something to aspire towards.

"She has smiled so much in her life that, even when she isn't smiling her face, somehow, still shines!"

Tuesday — June 23

BIRD song at twilight, the sun as it sets,
Surely this must be as good as it gets.
The day will now draw gently to its close
And the petals will fold on the pink briar rose.
Owls in their belfries will call to the night,
And bats will prepare for their nocturnal flight.
Mist patches will form in both woodland and lane,
A hint that tomorrow will be warm again.
So for the day that's been sunny and bright
Let's give thanks, as we wish one another "Good night".

Brian H. Gent

Wednesday — June 24

RAB and I were bemoaning the closure of another church and sharing memories of folk who used to attend it.

I described one man as someone who was "a big noise" in the church. Rab remembered him, but insisted that he himself had been a bigger noise. I asked him to explain.

"When I was an apprentice," Rab said, smiling wryly, "I fitted the clapper to the church bell."

Thursday — June 25

I'M telling it how it is!" was the first part of the conversation I overheard.

"Oh, really?" I heard Mary reply. "Well, I'm only telling it how it could be. Now, which would you prefer?"

Without hearing what was said, I knew the "how it is" was downbeat, uninspiring and leading nowhere. An excuse not to try.

But "how it could be"? That asks something of us. Usually that we try a little harder. And the world is regularly improved by those efforts.

I don't know which option Mary's friend chose. I had politely walked on by, pretending not to have listened. But I know which I prefer!

Friday — June 26

I HAVE been rereading "The Crackit Cup", a poetry collection by Scottish writer Irene Howat.

Her title refers to a character whose story runs through the collection. Tam is the crackit (cracked) cup. Irene refers to him as someone who "is still beautiful despite a little damage. The world is a better place for the likes of him."

None of us is perfect. The only difference is the degree of our brokenness. And a beautiful soul is a beautiful soul, no matter how it is presented.

Personally, I am glad of the crackit cups in my world, and grateful for those who see the beauty in them.

Saturday — June 27

COUNTRY people can be as set in their ways as anyone, perhaps more so on occasion.

Still, it was a farmer, having to adapt to the modern economy, who told me his grandfather had once warned against over-attachment to the past, saying, "There's no rock that the stream won't change."

"Tiny little pieces of that rock, worn down and broken away by the cold, unceasing flow of the hillside stream," the farmer offered thoughtfully. "Why, one day they might end up on a beach somewhere."

Sunday — June 28

FRIENDSHIP'S a flower for all seasons;
It never will fade away.
Lasting, with loyalty growing,
Bringing a joy to each day.
Friendship's a gift to be given,
For then you'll find – and it's true –
By passing it round, there's a promise
Very soon, it will come back to you!

Elizabeth Gozney

I N "The Tale Of Genji", an 11th-century Japanese romance, a young man discovers that the love of his life is to be married to someone else.

He sends her what is to be the last of many poems he has written for her.

After the poem is read out, the author of the tale adds, "The note containing this poem was attached to an ice-cold spray of bamboo, plucked from near the ground, and carried with such care that it was still coated with hoar-frost. The messenger was, on this as upon every other occasion, a person whose quality matched the elegance of the letter."

Very few doubt the quality – indeed, the beauty – of the message we, as people of faith, carry.

The question is, how well do we carry it?

How hard do we strive to make sure our qualities match that wonderful message?

Tuesday — June 30

A FRIENDLY greeting is a good thing, so why would it reduce anyone to tears?

Mary's good friend Beth had been hospitalised after a stroke. She recovered well, but the stroke took away her voice.

Weeks of frustration and writing on notepads followed.

Then Beth started being able to vocalise. She then began to say short, whispered words.

The other day Mary visited and was greeted with, "Hi, Mary. How are you?"

They were simple words, but Mary's tears flowed at the sound of them.

It is said that you never appreciate water until the well runs dry. Well, Mary had no idea how much she would miss a friendly greeting until she thought she would never hear it again – and then she did!

July

ORDINARILY, I'm not the biggest fan of habit. But not all habits are bad, and some are positively to be commended. Like, for instance, the one suggested by George Wilkinson, then Bishop of St Andrews, in the 1890s.

"Half a dozen lines of kindness," he wrote, "might bring sunshine into the whole day of some sick person."

What habit was he prompting us to develop? Sympathy, and doing something about it.

IN the early 1900s Ruth Jacobs – under the nom-de-plume of Wilhelmina Stitch – was know as "the poem-a-day lady". Why?

Because, in newspapers and magazines in Britain and Canada, she produced an uplifting poem for each day of publication.

A poem a day? Some of us struggle to find an uplifting thought for every day. But Ruth – Wilhelmina – proved that it can be done.

Wouldn't that be a habit worth cultivating?

IBN BATTUTA was a fourteenth-century Moroccan scholar and explorer. He spent thirty years travelling the known world, but only wrote about his experiences towards the end of his life. Why?

As he said, "Travelling . . . it leaves you speechless. Then it turns you into a story-teller."

Travel, by all means. But travel in wonder and appreciation. Then, later, share what you learned –- and enjoy the experience all over again!

Saturday — July 4

A PERSON might hear many a wise word and not be wise. So what would be the point of those words?

In the novel "David Elginbrod" by George MacDonald, Hugh has failed to benefit from sage advice, but MacDonald says those seeds of truth awaited only "the friendly aid of a hard winter, breaking up the cold, selfish clods of clay, to share in the loveliness of a new spring, and be perfected in the beauty of a new summer".

In other words, no word of truth or wisdom is ever wasted. They merely await the time they will be needed.

Sunday — July 5

WITHOUT our feathered friends, the birds, how sad the world would be,
They fill the sky with cheerful songs, they brighten every tree.
I love the chirping sparrows and the pigeons in the parks;
The blackbirds with their liquid song, the swans, the crows, the larks.
Our beaches would be miserable without a single gull,
And Christmas without robins in the snow would be so dull.
There's just one bird I wouldn't miss; I'd cheer if it were gone –
The cockerel on the farm next door that wakes me up each dawn!

Ewan Smith

Monday — July 6

THERE'S a place in Whitby where lots of people argue. Thankfully they are usually pretending; posing for the camera. Because, you see, the place is called Arguments Yard!

No-one really knows why it bears such an unusual name, although some think it may once have belonged to a Mr Argument.

I like the idea! Too often arguments spill over into other aspects of life or other relationships. Wouldn't it be more civilised if we had a specific place to argue, get things sorted out, and then we could leave that place, and any bad feeling, behind when we were done?

Our feathered friends fill
the sky with cheerful songs.

Tuesday — July 7

IN 1876, Ellen Harding Baker wanted to teach the people in her county about astronomy. Teaching aids were not very advanced in those days, and anyway were in very short supply.

So she stitched a beautifully detailed quilt of the solar system and carried it around with her, putting it on display at each lecture she gave.

Not only was that ingenious, it was also a wonderful example of working with what she had to hand. Remember, a lack of materials needn't stop you if you don't lack imagination.

Wednesday — July 8

I KNOW a man who has a collection of model trains in a display case fixed to his living-room wall. I know a woman who has a collection of jewellery in a box made of Kenyan soap-stone. I know a girl who has a collection of soft cuddly toys, well, everywhere!

Do you have a collection?

I like the notion the German Romantic writer Jean Paul Richter once had. He suggested we set aside time daily, or weekly, to reckon up the virtues of our belongings – of our wife, of our children – and contemplate them in a beautiful collection.

Do you have a collection? I sincerely hope you do.

Thursday — July 9

WE need, sometimes, to get away,
Leave cares behind, make tracks,
Seek out our piece of paradise,
And once again, relax.
These moments are quite precious,
And they bring an added plus,
If those we love and care about
Can share them, too, with us.

J. Darley

THE Poet Laureate's duty is to write about and record events that affect the nation in some way. But did you know that, for the past few years, there has been a pets' poet laureate?

It's not a dog who writes doggerel, or a cat who composes cute quatrains; it's a person writing about the role pets play in our lives, and the impact they have on us.

Is that going too far? Ask any pet owner and they'll tell you the relationship between person and pet is a beautiful thing. And well worth a verse or two, I'd say.

Saturday — July 11

AFTER World War II, the United States sent huge amounts of food and materials to help rebuild war-shattered Europe. Such inter-governmental deals could be a bit impersonal, and much of it would, eventually, be repaid.

To make it all a bit more personal and meaningful, a "Friendship Train" travelled across the States collecting gifts from individuals for the European people. This was then shipped across the Atlantic.

Two years later, the Merci Train made the return journey, carrying such personal items as the Europeans could spare for distribution across the States.

Gifts freely given in response to a need, and appreciation shown even in a time of hardship.

In desperate times, people are often at their most wonderful!

Sunday — July 12

I HOLD that a strongly marked personality can influence descendants for generations."

So wrote Beatrix Potter, who had no children of her own, but influenced many generations.

We might not write as many books, nor create as many loveable characters as Ms Potter did, but we, too, will have an influence. May it be a loving one.

WOULD you like to have fewer faults? The art critic and philanthropist John Ruskin suggested it might be best not to try to get rid of them.

His thinking went, "In every person who comes near, you look for what is good and strong; honour that; rejoice in it; and, as you can, try to imitate it; and your faults will drop off like dead leaves when their time comes."

In other words, cultivate the positive until there is no room for the negative.

Tuesday — July 14

IN the Philippines in the 1930s, a missionary wrote, "Never did I so feel the need of a silent typewriter as at this moment."

Why? Because the beauty of the countryside had him entranced. He wanted to describe it to people back home, but the clacking of the typewriter keys, he thought, ruined its tranquillity.

When we find those awe-inspiring places, or spiritually refreshing times, we usually can't help but talk about them. They are often too wonderful not to share.

But that doesn't mean we shouldn't tread softly, respecting the place, honouring the moment. Share, by all means, but in a way that doesn't spoil the gift.

Wednesday — July 15

THE little wooden platform by the lakeside was just big enough to accommodate a fisherman and his gear. But it was a heron eyeing the waters in the golden light of this particular morning, looking to break its fast.

A voice in my head said, "That's the way it ought to be. Everything we build should work equally well for man and nature."

Another voice laughed and said, "Tell that to the fish!"

They both had a point! But the second point needn't negate the first. Let's try to work with nature more often.

We all want to share awe-inspiring moments.

Thursday — July 16

THERE is a wood carving of an otter in a park that the Lady of the House and I like to visit. He appears to have caught the fish lying on the wooden "rock" in front of him.

As I watched, a two-year-old spotted it and toddled over. She looked closely, then stroked the otter's back. Then she kissed the otter's head. Then she kissed the fish. Then she went back to her mother.

It was just a beautiful moment. But, sometimes, that's enough!

Friday — July 17

THE writer O. Henry was dying. The sun was about to rise.

He said, "Turn up the lights, I don't want to go home in the dark."

The sun rose, turning the light up, and he did go home.

There isn't all that much we can control in our lives, but we can still write them with style; painting them more beautifully with the colours of our own personality.

Saturday — July 18

YOU might have heard the theory that if you are unhappy and you force yourself to smile, you will feel happier.

There's an approach to problems of the day that works along similar lines. Whatever your problem, this philosophy suggests you speak it out loud and add the words "and I love it" to the end.

For example, "It's raining outside, the dog needs walked, and I love it!", or "There isn't enough time in the day to do everything I have to do, and I love it!", always remembering to emphasise those last four words.

It may be that saying, "and I love it", or making ourselves smile, does have a positive effect on our emotions. Or perhaps we just feel like laughing at ourselves for our foolishness when we do things like that.

Either way . . .

SOME of us will have heard of, or perhaps even used, the expression "halcyon days". It conveys the idea of peace and plenty; relaxing, almost heavenly times.

So what does that have to do with kingfishers?

In ancient Greek legends, the halcyon – which is a type of kingfisher – would build its nest on the open sea. But before it did that, it used special powers to calm the patch of sea it wanted to build on.

It would then sit there in perfect tranquillity until its eggs hatched.

It's hard enough these days for us to believe that birds might do such things. It would be impossible to believe that humans could.

What we might do, however, is walk calmly into difficult situations or troubled relationships, find a place to "nest", then simply refuse to let that be anything other than a place of peace and love.

Those feelings will inevitably spread, and we might be able to have a few more halcyon days.

ANOTHER day beginning, Lord,
Who knows what it will bring?
Please keep me strong and cheerful, Lord,
And let my spirit sing.
So many are in need of love,
In need of comfort, too.
Please let me show them hope and joy,
A little kindness, too.
Another day ahead of me,
With battles I must win.
Lord, stay beside me all the way,
And give me strength within.

Iris Hesselden

Tuesday — July 21

OUR dear friend Mary is a church regular, and always has her Bible in hand when the minister reads scripture.

The minister is a younger fellow. He doesn't mind if people simply listen to him, or if they follow along with e-Bibles on their phones, but he's used to seeing Mary leafing through her old, well-worn, book.

When he saw her without it on Sunday, he couldn't help poking a little gentle fun.

"No Bible, Mary? Oh, dearie me, that's not like you."

"Oh," Mary replied a little airily. "I gave it to someone who needed it."

"People become very attached to their Bibles," the minister told me later. "But not for a second did I doubt she'd done just that. She's not one for keeping good news to herself."

Wednesday — July 22

YOU'RE looking very smart today," Mary said when she met me in the street.

"Thank you," I replied. "And you're . . ."

"Yes, thank you." She jumped into my hesitation. "I am, too. Oh, I didn't pay too much attention to the clothes I put on, but I looked out my finest appreciation, my best thankfulness, and my most stylish empathy this morning. And I dressed my mind in those."

Put like that, she may have been the best-dressed person I saw all day!

Thursday — July 23

ACCORDING to an encyclopaedia published in Galloway in 1824, "huam" is the noise an owl makes when it retires to the shade of the woods on sunny days.

Taking time to rest in the shade is just as important as enjoying the sun. Make sure to hum "huam" yourself now and again!

Friday — July 24

SHOULD the Lady of the House and I go visiting, we will usually take a gift for our hosts. It will be the normal sort of thing – flowers, sweets, a card. We will try to be as little trouble as possible.

The book publisher George Merriam, who lived and worked in the nineteenth century, imagined trouble personified, suggesting he might be a visitor to every house at one time or another.

Trouble, too, brings gifts, Merriam suggested. As he crosses your threshold, he will offer you "weakness, isolation, despair." But if you have the courage to look beyond that, you will see he holds in his other hand "fortitude, patience, self-control, wisdom, sympathy, faith."

Trouble won't wait to be invited in, but he will give you the gift you choose. Choose wisely.

Saturday — July 25

I HEAR people have experimented with talking harshly (and kindly) to plants. The result seems to be the same as when we speak to children. Harsh words inhibit growth, while kind words promote it.

I was interested to read James Allen's view on the matter, in his 1903 book "As A Man Thinketh". Mr Allen wrote that "right thinking begins with the words we say to ourselves".

Given all we know about the power of words, why would we speak to ourselves in anything other than an encouraging way? Yet we still do. Let's not.

If we speak kindly to ourselves, and grow as a result, imagine all we might then do for others.

Sunday — July 26

AS a good neighbour, Harry had enjoyed a busy week of helping. One neighbour declared him a hero, another her angel. He laughed those off, but took seriously the title bestowed by a neighbour who needed to talk.

She called him "a safe place".

BARBARA works in the city, though whenever she can she heads to the countryside.

She likes to visit different places, but, when work pressures get too much for her, she generally heads for one particular rocky hill.

Then she sits under a birch tree and her soul is refreshed.

"It's not the view," she told me. "It's the tree. You see, this fine tree grew out of a crack in a slab of granite on an exposed hilltop. It's difficult to imagine a harsher climate. When I find it difficult to keep going, I imagine the tree saying to me, 'You think you have it tough? Maybe you do. But growth is always possible. Even in the toughest of situations'."

SUNFLOWERS famously turn towards the sun. So it would have made sense for Greta to stand with the sun behind her when she photographed a field of them in the Dordogne.

Instead, she stood "behind" the field to take the picture.

Why? Because she wanted to capture the one sunflower, out of hundreds, which was stubbornly facing the wrong way.

I'm sure there is a horticultural reason for such contrariness, but it did remind me how lucky we are to have people in this world who will shine their light into the dark places where no-one looks.

THE Basque writer and philosopher Miguel de Unamuno believed there were two worlds.

"There is a world," he wrote, "the sensible world, which is the child of hunger, and there is another world, the ideal world, that is the child of love."

He believed we had the senses to see both worlds. Which one we saw most often depended entirely on which of the senses we exercised the most.

Which world would you most like to see?

MARY and I were discussing how generally wonderful life is and how there is probably so much more to it, spiritually, than we could ever begin to imagine.

At one point, I thought my dear friend had wandered completely off the conversational track.

"You know," she said, "there are creatures which live in the deepest seas, under such enormous pressure that if they were to rise towards the surface they might explode."

I didn't know how to reply to this, but I should have known that she would be making a point in her own unique way.

"Sometimes people are like that," she continued with a smile. "It's almost as if they are afraid to rise into the mysteries, towards a better understanding of it all.

"Perhaps they think it might change them. So they stay at the bottom, where it's familiar and safe."

What could I possibly add to that unexpected combination of philosophy and marine biology?

We won't explode; so rise.

ONE time, on an American game show, a woman told the audience that she had started that day by reading the "Love Chapter" of the Bible.

"Love is patient, love is kind," she said.

Then she substituted her own name for love, intending that she would be all of those good things.

When her husband got a question wrong and cost them some serious money, she – in front of the same audience – emphatically failed to live up to those ideals.

But you know what? She tried!

I don't know how many of us could live up to those expectations. But sometimes it is our failures that make us try harder the next time.

After all, "love always perseveres".

August

WHEN economists or market analysts make predictions, they often allow for a "margin of error". If their prediction lands somewhere in that zone, they reckon it a success.

You might expect people dealing with money to be specific and precise, but no, they usually give themselves some leeway.

When we are dealing with people, on the other hand, we are often much more demanding. We should have our standards and expectations, but it might be wise – and kind – always to allow others a decent margin of error.

After all, we might find ourselves in that margin from time to time!

STUDIES of some of the oldest cave paintings in the world suggest that they may have been made by "Neanderthal Man", meaning that they pre-date homo sapiens.

That means the urge to create art is older than our species! So, if the Neanderthals "invented" art, and we simply inherited it, where did they get the idea from?

Perhaps the urge to create is simply left over from the original Creation. Or perhaps Creation itself is an ongoing experience, and art is simply the best way we mortals can express how it feels being part of that experience.

Whatever it is, we need neither excuses nor deep philosophies to add our unique brushstrokes to the cosmic canvas. Paint, write, sculpt, craft. Or simply live your life like it's a work of art. Who are we to disagree with such a positive, beautiful, essential – and seemingly eternal – instinct?

Wouldn't that be a fine way to thank the greatest artist of all?

Live every day like
it is a work of art.

iStock.

Monday — August 3

IT is apparently the most popular course in Yale University's history. It's called "Psychology And The Good Life", and it has sections on acts of kindness, expressing gratitude, and creating and strengthening social connections.

You know . . . the things we used to call life, but from which the modern world seems to have isolated so many people.

If we aren't learning such things at our grandparents' knees any more, then I'll settle for them being taught in classes. The uptake of the course surely shows how important – and how worthwhile – they are.

Tuesday — August 4

WHEN Julius Caesar landed in Tunisia, legend has it that he fell on his face. The army behind him feared this was a bad omen, but Caesar stood and declared, "I take possession of thee, O Africa!"

Likewise, William the Conqueror is supposed to have fallen flat when he invaded England. Before this could unnerve his soldiers, he is supposed to have announced he had seized the land with both hands.

Now, I'm not suggesting we go invading places. I am, however, suggesting that when we fall, as we inevitably will, we will be in impressive company. And what matters most is not that we fell, but how we rose again.

Wednesday — August 5

I VISITED him in jail. The longer the visit lasted, the more I was convinced I should have stayed at home. There was nothing of repentance, nothing of remorse. Just defiance, justification and anger.

As I rose to leave, he growled, "How's my wife? And my wee boy?"

I sat down again. He had stepped out of his own way, opened a door, shown me what was behind his protective façade. And I was glad I had visited after all.

Thursday — August 6

THE article suggested that the impact of painful memories might be alleviated by writing them down, as if the written words could contain or take away some of the unpleasantness they can cause.

I can't speak to that, but the next day I bought a second-hand book. In it was an inscription from Alice, wishing her brother Willie a happy eightieth birthday. It was dated 1957.

I guess that both Alice and Willie have since gone to a better place. But I read her written words 60 years later, and I felt the love.

There may be something to the theory.

Friday — August 7

IN Gaelic poetry, the Great Hall of Scone in Perthshire was sometimes known as "Scone of the Noisy Shields".

When the King called for counsel, the earls would attend. Before the meeting began, they would hang shields emblazoned with their clan crests on the wall, and then beat them with their own weapons – the implication being that they would fight against their own interests for the sake of the King.

It's an idea that still resonates. As attached as we may be to our own ways, we should always be prepared to take a stand against them for a greater good.

Saturday — August 8

IN days gone by, an islander took a tourist out in his rowing boat. Noticing a different Gaelic word carved into each oar, the tourist asked about them.

The islander lifted one oar up, still paddling with the other. As the boat turned in a circle, he grunted, "Works!"

He lifted the second oar and resumed paddling with the first. As the boat turned in the opposite direction, he grunted, "Faith."

Smiling at the bewildered tourist, he added, "We need them both in the water, or we'll never reach the harbour."

Sunday — August 9

HE drives with his daughter in a child seat in the rear of the car. They chatter away through the journey and, from time to time, the three-year-old will say, "Daddy, look!"

His practised response is usually, "Do you really want me to look? Or would you rather I watched the road and kept us safe?"

It's a lesson that the world will have plenty of distractions for us, but we don't always need to pay attention to them.

"Finally, brothers and sisters, whatever is true, whatever is noble, whatever is right, whatever is pure, whatever is lovely, whatever is admirable – if anything is excellent or praiseworthy – think of such things." (Philippians 4:8.)

Monday — August 10

OUR dear friend Mary has been annoying people – in her own unique way!

When someone tells her a tale of woe, or of something gone wrong (unless it's something genuinely tragic), she listens, thinks, then asks them, "And how is this a gift?"

Her sincerity almost demands the person find an upside in what formerly seemed to be a purely negative thing. Sometimes they appreciate that; sometimes they get annoyed. Because, of course, some of us do like to complain more than we like to think.

But there are very few negative things to come into our lives that aren't – in some way – also positives. If only we take the time to identify just what the gift is.

Tuesday — August 11

I HEARD tell of, but have never seen, a church dedicated to all the saints. Many of the better-known saints are depicted in splendid stained-glass windows. Some carry religious symbols, some are shown carrying out the acts they are famous for, and, rendered in glass in amongst them, is a woman at a wash-tub.

Why? I don't think anyone really knows. But the most popular theory seems to be that not all saints have halos.

Wednesday — August 12

WHEN life seems bleak and grey, I recall that Robert Lloyd, chafing under the constraints of society, family and church, wrote to the poet Charles Lamb to complain that there was nothing sweet left in the world.

Lamb's reply pointed out that "roses and violets are yet in the earth." He followed this up with a list of things for which we ought to be thankful, ending with this thought:

"You may extract honey from every thing."

The world would be sweet if roses and violets were all it had. But even on the greyest day, it has so much more.

Thursday — August 13

PEOPLE who lived on farms or crofts far removed from towns and cities might have been familiar with the old advice, "Listen to the mountain winds until the streams abate."

There are times in life, like when the streams are full and impassable, where nothing much can be done. Being compelled to stay where you are, you might as well "listen to the mountain winds", or find some other beauty that, on busier days, you might have had less time to appreciate.

Friday — August 14

HARRY told me about a friend who was making some changes to his life.

"His day was spent in his house, his car or his office. Being so cut off from the world was taking its toll. I suggested he get some dirt on his hands."

I completely agreed with Harry's prescription while, at the same time, wondering why we said that, and why it worked.

"You do realise," Harry said with unquestionable confidence, "that 'heart' and 'earth' are made up of the same letters."

There was no logical connection. But somehow it made perfect sense.

Saturday — August 15

IT is traditionally described as "the lazy man's great burden".

What is it? Why, having to go to great lengths to avoid work, or having to come up with enough excuses not to help anyone.

A man or woman with any sense would see that some folk put more effort into not working than the work itself would require.

In many instances, doing the work is actually easier than avoiding it.

If you would carry an easier burden, be the busy person. And, if you are feeling charitable, pity the man who thinks he's getting off lightly, but isn't.

Sunday — August 16

THE path I walked had a slight incline, and the sun was low over the horizon. As I walked, I squinted more and more. I could only see a few feet in front of me. I was tempted to be annoyed.

To give my eyes a break, I turned around. The vista behind me was beautifully lit, and displayed by the same light I'd been complaining about.

To think I had walked through all of that glory and never really appreciated it!

The walk towards the light isn't easy. Growing closer to God might be a bit of a struggle. But the nearer you get to him, the greater will be the understanding and appreciation of all you've been through.

When you arrive at your destination, you will look back and see the journey was a glorious one.

Monday — August 17

AN old French saying suggests that "two men may meet, but two mountains never will." The suggestion is that inflating self-importance also isolates people – especially from others who think themselves similarly important.

Far better to stay humble and have friends.

DREAMING in the garden,
As work thoughts drift away,
The sun is calmly setting,
On the remnants of the day.
Still the glow of summer warmth,
From its last descent,
Lighting up the roses,
As its final rays are spent.
Restful green around us,
Birdsong bids goodnight,
Breathing in the blissful peace,
Welcoming twilight.
On this sleepy, gentle evening,
Our words are softly said,
Marvelling in creation
Before thoughts turn to bed.

Linda Brown

WE might talk of common sense not being so common, or happiness being in short supply, but author William George Jordan thought something else was "the rarest quality in human life".

Can you guess what it was?

In a book published at the turn of the 20th century, he gave that title to calmness.

Calmness, he insisted, was not the same as fatalism or disengagement. He thought calmness was at its most majestic when fully engaged in all the tides and trials of life.

I'm inclined to agree.

Think of all the things that might unbalance our equilibrium, that might change our mood against our will, then firmly decide not to let them.

Be the calm in life's storm.

Ancient, yet timeless.

St Mary's Church, Whitby.

iStock.

Thursday — August 20

THE writer J.M. Barrie wrote about forcing open a jammed drawer. It took a lot of effort, and, inevitably, what he was looking for wasn't there.

But from the back of the drawer fell some pages of the original manuscript of "Peter Pan", which he had completely forgotten were there.

Our lives are not short of the equivalents of stuck drawers, or fruitless searches. Neither are they short of the unexpected – but delightful – surprises that use those seemingly frustrating times to pop into our world.

Friday — August 21

WILLIAM MULOCK lived a busy life. A member of the Canadian parliament, he was also a lawyer, businessman, judge, vice-chancellor of a university and a philanthropist.

On his eighty-sixth birthday, he might have been forgiven for dwelling in the past.

Instead, he wrote, "The rich spoils of memory are mine. Mine, too, are the precious things of today: books, flowers, pictures, nature, and sport . . . The best thing of all is friends. The best of life is always further on. Its real lure is hidden from our eyes, somewhere behind the hills of time."

Saturday — August 22

ANCIENT, yet timeless
This image I keep
Of the church and the churchyard
Where centuries sleep.
Of the glowing, arched windows
The clock-face, the steeple,
And the sweet country faith
Of God's faithful people.

J. Darley

Sunday — August 23

JOHN WESLEY was touring the north of England – and generally being disapproved of – when he arrived at a Newcastle inn around ten in the evening.

"Some to whom we spoke at our inn were very attentive," he wrote. "But a gay young woman waited on us, quite unconcerned. When we went away, she fixed her eyes, and neither moved nor said one word, but appeared as much astonished as if she had seen one risen from the dead."

When you speak of God, you needn't concern yourself overmuch with who is or isn't paying attention. God knows who he wants to hear your words.

Monday — August 24

PEOPLE who have completed walking pilgrimages are the best sources of advice if you are planning something similar.

They can tell you the best guidebooks and favourite places to stop.

Of course, the advice will differ depending on the journey, but "travel light" and "take care of your feet" are examples that will frequently come up.

I could say the same – with only a slight difference – were I to view this life as a pilgrimage. Travel light, and take care of your soul.

Tuesday — August 25

A GREEN energy company has established a solar energy farm inside the Chernobyl exclusion zone.

They say they wanted to make a positive difference in an area that has suffered more than most from man's folly.

Reclaiming even a small part of a place burned out by a nuclear meltdown . . . Wow!

Now, tell me, what is that situation in your life that is so bad you can't make it even a little bit better?

Wednesday — August 26

WE use the term "as good as my word" to imply honesty. Someone has given their word, and they will stand by it.

But did you ever wonder how good your words actually are? Not your oath or your promise, but the words you use in everyday speech. Is your conversation peppered with negatives or superlatives, disparagement or encouragement, problems or solutions?

The words we use reflect the way we live. More than that, they impact the people who listen to them.

Be as good as your word when it comes to keeping promises. And the rest of the time? Be as good as your words, having made sure they were the best possible words for the occasion.

Thursday — August 27

HUMAN beings have a way of complicating things, but the truth is often simple.

Like these words from Leo Tolstoy:

"Let us forgive each other – only then will we live in peace."

Can you imagine the difference it would make if we did?

Friday — August 28

IT was in a frame, it had a price tag and it was on the wall of a gallery.

Someone must think it art, I thought to myself. But it was simply a collection of swirled coloured threads and little pieces of fabric.

As I moved away, I heard a woman say, "Call that art? Looks like the bottom of my granny's sewing basket!"

I lingered to hear her husband, but he was silent for a moment.

"When I was wee," he eventually said in a wistful voice, "the bottom of my granny's sewing basket was one of the most fascinating, creative, beautiful things I ever saw."

So art it is, then.

Granny's sewing basket:
fascinating and creative.

Saturday — August 29

HAVE you ever heard the expression "dog tired"? For most of us it might simply mean exhausted, done in, unable to do or give any more.

But Sheriff Alexander Nicolson of Kirkcudbright, some time around 1881, wrote, "No animal wearies himself so unsparingly as a dog; none is so ready, when most weary, to obey his master's call."

Noble beasts, some undoubtedly are. We might be as fine – even though we are dog tired – if only we had something or someone we loved as much as a dog loves its master.

Sunday — August 30

HE decided to try to line up his actions with the will of God about every fifteen minutes or half an hour. Other people to whom he confessed his intention said it was impossible.

"I judge from what I have heard that few people are trying even that," wrote the missionary Frank Laubach.

Impossible? Perhaps. But, what's to be lost by trying? Start with once a day.

Monday — August 31

DAD had taken his children – all under twelve – to a café to recharge their batteries. They still wore their numbers from a nearby cross-country run.

As they passed, I asked, "Was it a good run?"

The two older ones nodded politely and said it had been.

The third child, being younger, cared less about politeness.

"I got up early this morning," she told me, "and I still came in last."

Dad explained there had been a big turn-out.

"Ah," I sympathised. Then I added, "But you still beat the hundreds of thousands of people who stayed in their beds."

"I never thought of that!" she said brightly, recharged more by the thought, it seemed, than the breakfast she had just finished.

September

I HAVE no idea what the radio programme was about, but in it they mentioned a school child with emotional difficulties being instantly calmed by an unexpected encounter with a friendly dog.

Do you know what friendly dogs have going for them? What works the calming miracle in our souls?

They have no expectations of us. They never judge us.

A cynic might say they are just after a treat. But that only means they understand that if you're happy, they'll be happy, too.

No expectations. No judgement. An interest in the happiness of others, for the good that it does the world.

We might learn a thing or two from friendly dogs.

AN ancient Japanese romance tells of two young lovers, separated by their circumstances, who communicate via music.

The man plays his flute from the lakeside, and his sweetheart joins in from her room, accompanying him on her zither.

The writer thought it worth mentioning that her zither was "tuned to the autumn-mode".

No doubt this reflected her sadness, but . . .

Sometimes we spend so much time regretting the season that has just passed, or looking forward to a season's return, that we don't have time to tune into the season that is actually here.

Each of them has its own "music", its own unique delights.

We can ignore that fact, or we can tune in to the season, and accompany it with the music it inspires in us.

Thursday — September 3

A CHIEF, during one of Scotland's many wars, decided to take his men into the fray. But to get there, they had to walk through glens populated by supporters of the other side.

Legend has him saying, "We will take the high road. Let them take it ill or well."

How they took it isn't known, but the same dilemma might occur any time we take a stand for the right, honourable and good. There will be people who have different priorities.

Take the high road and let the others take it as they will.

Who knows? They might end up taking it with you.

Friday — September 4

THEY say that, in days when railway stations had porters, the porter's trick was "a little load – and frequent". By making it look like he was doing more, he might hope to earn a greater tip.

It's a cynical view, and not one likely to be appreciated by the porter himself. Given that he would then have to help the next traveller, and the next, he had a vested interest in ensuring he didn't strain or injure himself.

Those of us struggling with more than our fair share of heavy loads might remember the porter's trick. Don't try to handle everything at once. Deal with one issue, and, only after it's done, look to the next.

A little load and frequent. It will get you safely to where you need to be.

Saturday — September 5

I DO enjoy definitions of love. This old verse may benefit from being sung in its original Gaelic, but it is worth sharing in its translated form:

"Paramours' love is like the sea's flowing tides.
Wayfarers' love is like the north wind off a rock.
But married folks' love is like a ship sailing to harbour."

Sunday — September 6

I WISH there was a staircase, a staircase shining bright,
To lead us from the darkness, to take us to the light,
To guide us ever onwards, right up to heaven's door,
To meet again our loved ones and hold them close once more.
If sighs could make a staircase, I'd build it without fail,
If wishes could achieve it – but wishes are too frail.
Yet somehow deep inside me, faith cannot be dismissed
That bonds 'twixt earth and heaven most truly do exist.
For love can make a staircase; a bridge that will not break,
And love can keep us hopeful, however hearts may ache.
And when at last the day comes I, too, have reached my time,
I know I'll find that staircase, and then, with joy, I'll climb.

Maggie Ingall

Monday — September 7

THERE'S no getting away from it. Life can be difficult. Sometimes, it breaks even the strongest of us. And we tend to think of broken things as being worthless, don't we?

But go to any museum. There's a good chance, especially in the larger museums, that amongst their most cherished and valuable items will be some Greek or Roman mosaics.

And what are mosaics made of? Broken things. Pieces of stone or glass, broken into small pieces, but arranged artistically.

Next time you are feeling a little broken, pick up the pieces of your life and think, "How might I put them together again, in a new, and more beautiful, design?"

Tuesday — September 8

IT'S a short, anonymous, verse I found on a sheet of newspaper from the turn of the 20th century. May I repeat it here for the good it might do?

"How oft a gleam of glory sent, straight through the deepest darkest night,
Has filled the soul with heavenly light, with holy peace and sweet content."

HOW precious is life? Or should I ask, is it cheap enough that we might waste large swathes of it complaining and being unappreciative?

When John Richard Green could no longer carry out church duties, he became a librarian, and compiled a history of the English people.

He wrote, "What seems to grow fairer to me as life goes by is the love and grace and tenderness of it; not its wit and cleverness, but just the laughter of little children, friendship, the cosy talk by the fireside, the sight of flowers and the sound of music."

Appreciation like that is something many of us hope we will achieve in old age. Until then, we continue to grumble. John Richard Green died in 1883, aged forty-five.

Thursday — September 10

THERE was a storm last night, but that didn't stop Harry going for his morning walk early the next day.

"How was it?" I asked.

"Well, the path was blocked in five different places by fallen trees. But for the person who might have come after me, it was only blocked by three!"

He's too old to be shifting trees, which is probably why he left three. But his point was taken. Whichever path you take through life, make sure to leave it better for those who come after.

Friday — September 11

WHEN Dorothy is trapped by the tornado in the movie version of "The Wizard Of Oz", a window frame knocks her unconscious. When she wakes, she finds herself in the wonderful land of Oz.

In L. Frank Baum's book, however, Dorothy resolves "to wait calmly and see what the future would bring". Then she makes her way to bed – across a pitching, tilting floor – and goes to sleep!

One approach makes for a more exciting film. The other makes for a more peaceful life.

Saturday — September 12

IT is said there are more than four thousand registered designs of tartan. The distinctive patterns traditionally represented different families or clans, so a lot of thought, tradition and pride goes into them.

But a wise Highlander is supposed to have remarked, "The tartan is all of one stuff." Meaning that behind the colours, the craft, the expense, was almost always wool.

Many things differentiate us as people, but we might remember the same sage advice. We are all of one stuff.

Sunday — September 13

PERHAPS they weren't used to this style of communion. The bread had been passed around, and everyone had eaten. The minister asked that we wait until everyone had received one of the silver cups filled with communion wine before partaking together.

The young man received his and drank it. As he realised what he had done, he blushed and turned to the young woman at his side. She smiled and poured half of her blessed sacrament into his cup. Then they drank, together, with the rest of the church.

From the few words we had exchanged, I gathered they were only recently wed. But I have high hopes for the communion of their marriage.

Monday — September 14

THE orchard has a stand where it sells the apples that aren't "pretty" enough to go to the shops. The sign says, *We've had troubles. We've fallen. One thing or another prevented us from being all we could be. But underneath all of that, we are still delicious!*

The man in front of me read the sign and muttered, "Oh, I know what you mean!" Then he dropped six less-than-perfect apples into a paper bag.

I imagine he enjoyed them more than any he might have bought in a supermarket.

Tuesday — September 15

AS well as Great-aunt Louisa's diaries, the Lady of the House has in her possession an old jewellery box.

The items inside were gathered by Louisa from various family members and, lacking her knowledge, we can only guess which ring, which bracelet or which earrings belonged to which relative.

I am particularly fond of the delicate gold ring that hides the inscription, *Be to his virtues very kind. Be to his faults a little blind.*

Why? Perhaps because I am glad someone shows me the same grace. And because I think we might do worse than employ the same philosophy with everyone we meet.

Wednesday — September 16

DR SAMUEL JOHNSON wrote, "As it is said of the greatest liar, that he tells more truth than falsehood; so it may be said of the worst man, that he does more good than evil."

That conclusion may not always be a true one, but for the majority of us, having to deal with such people in our day-to-day lives, it is certainly an aid to forgiveness.

Thursday — September 17

A WRITER sent a copy of his newly published first novel to an old friend.

Shortly afterwards he received the message: "Good to hear from you. Hope you are well. Thanks for the book. There's a spelling mistake on the fourth line of the thirty-seventh page. Best wishes."

Doubtless, the friend thought he was being helpful. But, perhaps subconsciously, he was more concerned with showing how smart he was than with actually helping.

Faults may need pointing out so they can be corrected. But would it have taken away from that to add, "The other 59,999 words were spelled perfectly and beautifully arranged"?

A jewellery box can hold more than heirlooms.

Friday — September 18

THE Taiwanese village had been a home for families of veterans. But, as property prices soared, they were bought for development.

When only 11 houses remained, the government wanted to knock them down.

Using his own money, Huang Yung-Fu started painting the houses. He painted animals, celebrities, sports stars; he painted the roof tiles different colours, he painted flowers on the paths.

And he kept painting.

Five years after he first picked up his brushes, the government told him they wanted to make the village – which now attracts a million visitors a year – an area of cultural significance.

Who says one person can't make a difference?

Saturday — September 19

SPEED records are being set and broken all the time: on land, on sea, in the air. Generally, we try to go faster.

But in 1929, the poet Wilhelmina Stitch suggested something a little different:

"Here is a record that is hard to beat; never too fast for those with injured wings; never too fast for those with weary feet; never too fast for little humdrum things that must be done for someone else's sake; never too fast to hear a brother's voice; just slow enough, as we our journey take, to see the signpost, 'Beauty', and rejoice."

Sunday — September 20

YOU might not get many people popping in," the minister said, "but I am sure Jesus visits regularly."

"He does not," the parishioner retorted.

"Oh!" the surprised minister said.

"How can he 'visit' the house where he already lives?"

"Ahh!"

126

Monday — September 21

S.R. CROCKETT was a Scottish writer of children's stories in the late 1800s. In the introduction to his collection "Sweetheart Travellers", he laments the fact that the tales are not as "full of the glint of spring flowers when they are wet and the sun shines sideways on them" as they might have been.

His reason for this was that he had "grown too far from the grass and the good smell it used to give when it came well-nigh to my knees."

I suggest that when we feel we have grown too far from the grass, we bend those knees. That smell and glint are too precious to lose.

Tuesday — September 22

INSPIRED by his uncle Pepin, who was famous for his fabulous stories, the Czech author Bohumil Hrabal coined the term *pábatelé* in a 1964 book by the same name.

It translates as "palaverers", but for Hrabal it meant someone who didn't care to distinguish between fantasy and reality, preferring, instead, to look for the beauty in everything.

I'm not sure I agree with the implication that seeing beauty in everything is so fantastical. Wonderful, yes, but surely not a fantasy. Not if we look close enough. Not if we understand well enough.

People like Uncle Pepin – the *pábatelé* – might cause the rest of us to stop and wonder. And, perhaps, change how we look at the world.

Wednesday — September 23

WHEN Malala Yousafzai was fifteen years old, she received death threats for going to school. Her response was, "I think of it often . . . Even if they come to kill me, I will tell them what they are trying to do is wrong, that education is our basic right."

Recently, a five-year-old girl in Ayrshire, thousands of miles from Malala's home in Pakistan, told me she had learned in class about the girl who was shot for going to school, but didn't die.

Education. So much more powerful than guns.

Thursday — September 24

IT would be foolish to pretend that life had no difficulties, or that, if it did, a cheery disposition could overcome them all. It would be worse than foolish, though, to convince ourselves that those difficulties were the greater part of life.

The poet Elizabeth Barrett Browning put it like this: "There are nettles everywhere, but smooth green grasses are more common still; the blue of heaven is larger than the cloud."

Nettles can be cut and clouds eventually blow away.

Friday — September 25

DO you remember the labels on the insides of school books? The student would write their name there, the date, and the condition of the book.

When Tom was given "The Land Of Romance And Adventure", he said its condition was "Rotten". Two years later, Hugh recorded it as "Terrible".

Sixty years later, it sits on my shelf – still intact, glue and tape having been delicately applied where it needed them most.

Who did that, I couldn't say. But after Hugh, Sarah added her name to the record. She declined to comment on the book's condition.

Perhaps she simply settled for making it a better one.

Saturday — September 26

PATRICIA ST JOHN was a writer, house mother and a WWII nurse. She knew a thing or two about deserts, having served as a Christian missionary in north Africa.

She once wrote of God, "When He plans to plant a garden, He starts in the desert."

In other words, for God to create a new thing, he starts with the absence of that thing and builds anew.

In the same vein, we might ask where the "deserts" of friendship and love are in our lives and our relationships. And then set about making those places flower.

Enjoy life's green grass.

The Peak District.

THERE'S a joke about a woman who buys a magnolia tree from a garden centre. She takes it home, plants it, feeds it with nutrients. It looks good.

A few weeks later, it seems to start wilting. Then its leaves start falling off.

She gathers up some of the leaves and seals them in a bag. Then she takes them back to the garden centre and demands the owner carry out a scientific examination of them to see what her poor tree was suffering from.

"Oh, I don't need a microscope for this," he says. "I know exactly what's wrong with your magnolia tree!"

"What is it?" she asks.

"Autumn," is the answer.

The changing of the seasons reminds us that there are many, many things outwith our control. But we needn't worry, because they are still under control.

God's control.

MARY ANN EVANS knew how other people's opinions could hurt. She adopted the pen-name of George Eliot because she knew people would not take her work seriously if they thought it composed by a woman.

She also wrote, "While we are coldly discussing a man's career, sneering at his mistakes, blaming his rashness, and labelling his opinions . . . that man, in his solitude, is perhaps shedding hot tears because his sacrifice is a hard one, because strength and patience are failing him to speak the difficult word, and do the difficult deed."

Until we know everything about a person – which arguably we never will – we should err on the side of kindness when we speak to them.

You never know.

Tuesday — September 29

OUR dear friend Mary has several sets of babushka (or matryoshka) dolls. Each doll will have five, or sometimes seven, others like it nestled inside.

With each coming from the preceding one, it's a cute way of representing the generations of a family.

The designs sometimes make historical or political points, but the most common designs are simple, little mother-figures.

I say "simple", but Mary put me right on that score.

Taking a set I had thought nothing of from the shelf, she explained: "The outer one wears a headscarf. That symbolises protection. The next one's apron signifies home. The third has a chicken, which means happiness. The fourth is holding a dove, the sign for heaven. The fifth has a bouquet of flowers, meaning times of plenty."

Protection, home, happiness, heaven, plenty. What mother wouldn't want to pass those on to the generations to come?

Wednesday — September 30

THE summer brought us happy days
In spite of storms and rain,
And now September touches hearts
As memories remain.
The summer brought the harvest, Lord,
The gifts which you bestow,
And autumn paints the hills and trees
To leave a warming glow.
The gifts of life are ours to share
With people far and near,
But most of all the gift of hope
Each season of the year.
Be with us, Lord, through all the weeks,
Whatever comes along,
And keep within our hearts and minds
Our own September song.

Iris Hesselden

October

FOLLOWERS of Islam pray five times a day. Would that be an inconvenience? Adoniram Judson, an American missionary serving in Burma, recommended we "endeavour seven times a day to withdraw from business and company" to offer up our souls. Too much?

I would not hesitate to recommend taking time away from the hustle and bustle to reconnect with the Divine, or simply to remember you are loved, for the good it undoubtedly does. But how often?

Well, if you have a mobile phone, I guess you will recharge it at least once a day. Perhaps more often. Why would you treat your own "battery" – your soul – with less care? Plug in!

THANK you for being there for me,
To lend a listening ear;
For helping me to understand,
And helping fog to clear.
Thank you for your kindness;
It means so much to me,
Knowing I can lean on you
For advice and honesty.
Thanks for all the little things
You've done without a care.
I'm not sure what I would have done
If you had not been there.
Thank you doesn't seem enough,
But at least it's a start,
And know, these words of gratitude,
They come straight from my heart.

Carrie Hewlett

Saturday — October 3

THERE once was a miller called Ewen who lived on the banks of the River Dee. Somehow, he displeased royalty and gave rise to a saying in the area: "The King doesn't care for Ewen, and Ewen cares not whether or no."

And why should a miller care what a king thought? If he has grain coming in from the farmers and flour going out to the bakers, he is playing his part in keeping people fed.

It's nice to have everyone think you wonderful. It rarely happens, though. And, so long as you are playing your part in something good, and playing it well, then you needn't care what others think.

Sunday — October 4

A FRIEND was walking through the autumn mist towards her bee hive when she had an unexpected encounter with a deer. Their eyes met and their souls seemed to mingle.

"It was like seeing God," she said. "Who is always there, of course. We just don't always remember to look."

I see deer regularly when out dog-walking, and I said so to a man who works in the single building in the area.

"There are no deer around here," he told me, contradicting all I had just said. "I've worked here for five years and I've never seen any."

Some don't look because they have never been shown; some because it might challenge their world view.

But the deer were there, all the same.

Monday — October 5

WHICH is sharper, a razor blade or an axe? A razor blade, I would guess. But which would you use to cut down a tree?

When we are judging something – or someone – as we so often do, remember that the standard we are measuring them against might have nothing to do with the unique gift or purpose they offer to the world.

Tuesday — October 6

JEREMY'S wife, Geri, recently had an operation to her foot. When I asked how she was doing, he replied, "She's hobbling well."

The fact that she was hobbling was the starting point for Jeremy, and he was more concerned with (and more proud of) how well she was doing it. I liked that.

In a world where it seems that everyone has some hidden trial, or some sorrow they are bearing, we might all be said to be "hobbling".

Whatever it may be that you are dealing with, if you are doing so with grace, with courage and with hope for the future, then, like Geri, you are hobbling well. And I am proud of you!

Wednesday — October 7

WITH long nights and dull days, just getting out of bed in the morning can be a chore. We might bemoan the duties that have our feet hitting the bedroom floor, but . . .

Charles Kingsley, author of "The Water Babies", wrote, "Thank God every morning, when you get up, that you have something to do that day which must be done, whether you like it or not."

That "something" will have its own purpose, but its secondary task – that of making us available for the blessings and rewards the day has to offer – has so much more potential.

The day awaits!

Thursday — October 8

YOU are young, my son," Plato wrote in his Laws, "and, as the years go by, time will change and even reverse many of your present opinions. Refrain therefore awhile from setting yourself up as a judge of the highest matters."

Some might think themselves not so young and therefore entitled to fixed opinions. But, while there are still years ahead, while there is more experience to be gained, the smarter option might be to keep on learning.

DO you enjoy having others laugh at you? Does anyone? But it's a very different thing to laugh at yourself.

Priest Henri de Tourville, who lived in France in the 19th century, was a man of the church, but he was also a sociologist, philosopher and educator.

He said, "It is a splendid habit to laugh inwardly at yourself. It is the best way of regaining your good humour and of finding God without further anxiety."

WHAT'S the only flag the British Navy flies higher than its national flag? The Worship Pennant, indicating prayer time or religious services are underway.

The Royal Navy's Worship Pennant was created when England and Holland were at war and is composed of emblems from both countries.

So, at times of prayer, it was possible to fly the enemy's banner.

This Sunday, if you can, why not lay aside enmity and division and sit a while in unity, under the One who is above all flags and greater than all divisions?

IN a book dated 1864 and by a poet identified as W.B.R., I found: "One sat at an instrument and played. Three listened to what the music said as they might have done to the song of a bird. But, oh, what different things they heard!"

The poet went on to describe the mind of each listener as a prism, stained with their own sins, joys, loves, regrets. The same music went into their ears, but the way it reached their hearts depended on the lives they had led.

I would agree – and take the thought a little further. The prisms of our minds may be stained, but meditating on God will go a long way towards washing them clean again.

Monday — October 12

THINK – I hope – I am a helpful man. But this person, with their unique collection of problems, I was tempted, to my shame, to walk on by.

Then someone else, someone already struggling with a load that would have broken many, sat down with them, listened to them, and asked how they could help.

Why do we suffer in life? Why do we put rough gold in a crucible and burn it? Purity! Beauty!

Some of us go through the fire. The rest of us just watch in wonder.

Tuesday — October 13

IN Plato's "Symposium", the philosopher Diotima refers to the student "who has been instructed thus far in the things of love."

Now, you and I know something of the depth and beauty of love. More than that, we know what love adds to a life, to a family, to a community. And yet our world leaders often seem to discount it as a way of making things better. Studies will be done and experts will be consulted before they go about their usually less than loving way.

Imagine if love had the same stature as statistics or economics. Imagine if it was studied as a science. What could we not achieve?

Wednesday — October 14

APPLE, damson, plum or pear,
Harvest home and time to share.
Kitchen filled with smells so nice:
Fresh-chopped fruit and fragrant spice,
Pickles sharp, and chutney sweet.
Home-made jam, a tasty treat,
Gifts for neighbours, gifts for friends,
Nature's bounty never ends.
Some for you and some for me –
Perfect for a fireside tea!

Maggie Ingall

Nature's bounty never ends.

LAKE TAHOE in Nevada is known for its crystal-clear waters. It would be a fun thing to experience from any kind of boat, but these days visitors can paddle it in see-through canoes. The boating trip becomes a more amazing experience by changing the boat.

Likewise, if we want to experience something new, or something more profound, we can only go so far as we are. In our old boats, so to speak. If we want to experience life more clearly, more deeply, then we can't remain as we always were. We need to allow the experience to change us. And change us.

Friday — October 16

MODERN technology has reached the point where it is perfectly possible to fall out with someone you have never met. One such online friend had put me down the previous evening, but a good night's sleep had provided me with the perfect, stinging comeback.

I fired up my computer, all set to continue the argument.

But the first few posts from other people on my social media feed were, well, beautiful!

So, I thought, "Maybe I should go that way instead."

And the argument stopped right there.

All of which will tell you two things. The first is that I am fickle. The second is that you will never know all the good the beauty and kindness you put out into the world will do.

And isn't that the best reason to do more of them?

Saturday — October 17

ANNE'S son recently became her official carer, a situation that annoys her more than a little. Why? Because when he accompanies her to her hospital visits, the nurses now get a run-down of how she has been feeling rather than her customary, "Oh, I'm fine!"

As a result, her health care is improving.

What a blessing is someone who loves us enough to annoy us!

Sunday — October 18

THE Irish poet and hymnist Thomas Moore wrote in his Ballad Stanzas: "I knew by the smoke that so gracefully curled, above the green elms that a cottage was near. And I said, 'If there's peace to be found in the world, a heart that is humble might hope for it here'."

If one had travelled long on foot, or on horseback, a roof for the night and a fire for warmth might seem the most exquisite blessings. In times of ease and plenty, however, they might be dismissed as paltry offerings.

I tend to believe our homes in heaven will be simple places, like that unseen cottage. But the increased appreciation in our hearts will make them seem like palaces.

Monday — October 19

A GROUP of teens were planning a European holiday and they wanted to share something of their South Sea Islands culture while they were there. The trouble was, they lived in Australia, were two or three generations removed from the islands, and didn't know anyone who still did the traditional dances.

So they asked around, they researched, and they recreated dances that had their UK audiences entranced.

A thing isn't gone until it's forgotten. And a beautiful thing will always be worth reviving. What would you bring back?

Tuesday — October 20

IT was a framed ink sketch of a "Lady Bountiful" figure in an antiques shop. The caption beneath it might have been a quote from a book or a line of a poem. It read, "She put sovereigns in our hands and told us they were sixpences."

It struck me two ways. The first was that people who do good from a pure heart will generally try to downplay it. The second was that those who give from genuine kindness actually give far more than the value of the coin or the deed itself.

Wednesday — October 21

AT this time of year, we aren't short of rainy days. We might be tempted to think of them as nuisances to be avoided. But an anonymous poet in an issue of "Harper's Weekly" from 1865 describes the autumnal mist, the wintry rain and the springtime shower as providence sent from heaven to Earth. In the poem, called "Blessed To Give", they bring with them a message worth repeating.

"All whisper soft, to seed and flower, 'We know no other life to live but this. We give'."

Thursday — October 22

HER dad annoyed her. He had annoyed her most of her adult life. She didn't understand why he couldn't just be more loving.

I let her vent her frustrations. Then I mentioned a charity fund-raiser she had recently completed. Her total had been reached in record time with the help of a sizeable anonymous donation.

"I thought that was you," she confessed. But further investigation revealed the anonymous donor had, in fact, been her dad.

"I don't know what to make of that," she told me.

Perhaps we might make of it that people often have difficulty showing love in a way that matters to us, but it doesn't necessarily mean they aren't trying!

Friday — October 23

THE ancient Chinese had a fine way of incorporating truths in fables. I particularly like the tale of Chen Xiao. One evening he saw his neighbour moving the fence that divided their property. Under cover of darkness he claimed some of Chen Xiao's land.

The next day, reasoning the neighbour must need the extra space, Chen Xiao moved the fence even further into his land. The neighbour, who had been motivated by greed, was so touched that he moved the fence back beyond where it had originally been, giving Chen Xiao more land than he started off with.

It doesn't always work out like that, but it does often enough to make generosity always the best option.

Saturday — October 24

THE preacher and novelist George MacDonald had an uplifting take on tasks or duties we might not be looking forward to. He suggested that if we had an unpleasant duty to perform at noon, we ought not to let it cast its shadow over nine o'clock, ten o'clock or eleven o'clock.

Instead you should, "do the work of each and reap your reward in peace. So, when the dreaded moment in the future becomes the present, you shall meet it walking in the light, and that light will overcome its darkness."

Sunday — October 25

NIKOS KAZANTZAKIS, in his philosophical novel "Report To Greco", wrote, "I said to the almond tree, 'Sister, speak to me of God.' And the almond tree blossomed."

If we truly believe God loves us and wants only the best for us, then how can we, in that knowledge, do anything other than flourish? We won't need to speak. Others will look at us and know we are loved! Such blossom will be our gospel.

Monday — October 26

THE archway seemed to have been built without any mortar fixing the rough stone blocks together. It was beautiful – and impossible.

Until the keystone was put in place at the top of the arch, the builder would surely have relied on a wooden frame to keep everything up in the air. Once the keystone was in, the frame would have been broken down. The archway was only possible because of support that had been there when it was needed, and taken away when it wasn't.

The beauty of the construct outlasted the structure that caused it to be.

Isn't it a wonderful thought that, out there, long after we have forgotten the times we were supportive, the results of our support might still be standing?

I TOOK a slow evening perambulation with an elderly golden retriever. We walked the same path.

My ears tingled with the onset of a good frost and I doubt her fur-covered ears even felt it. I was almost dizzy from looking up at the half-moon-lit, crystal-clear sky, plotting constellations and identifying planets. She had her head down, exploring the world through its scents.

We were on very different walks.

It's perhaps no surprise that a dog and a man should see the same thing differently. But it might surprise some that two men, or two women, might also have as wide a gap in their understanding of their similar lives.

I will never be able to appreciate that walk like a dog. My nose isn't up to it. But what I can do, and what will make my world immeasurably richer, is stop deciding my version of any experience is the only one, and learn to appreciate the value of different points of view.

Wednesday — October 28

WHEN the Polynesian islanders first caught sight of the sails of European ships on the horizon, they thought something magical was happening. Whether that was a happy encounter or not can still be debated.

But the islanders later described the sailors as "the men who had burst through the heavens".

Of course, they hadn't; they had voyaged around the world, but those white sails against the blue might have looked like holes in the sky; like heaven bursting through.

The world seems a smaller place these days, but does heaven still burst through?

It depends on how you look. For some, heaven bursts through every time the sun rises, every time a child laughs, every time a flower opens or a snowflake forms.

The Polynesians looked to the horizon. Where do you look for heaven breaking through?

Thursday — October 29

A DAY where the wind seemed determined to take the breath from my cheeks reminded me of an old English proverb.

"'Sail!' said the King. 'Hold!' said the wind."

It reminds us that even the most powerful must occasionally bend to a higher power – and they are, doubtless, the better for it.

Friday — October 30

FIVE-YEAR-OLD Amelia was excited to tell me about her gymnastics display. She had been really upset after getting one move wrong. But she was delighted that she had helped two other girls when they needed it.

She's been learning "sums" at school, so she was able to tell me, "Two goods, take away one bad, equals one good. So, I'm happy!"

Every life has ups and downs. We all make mistakes, but we also help where we can. And even if the sum total of our life only adds up to "one good" then it will still have been worthwhile.

We can still be happy!

Saturday — October 31

I READ an old short story called "The Unkind Word". Next to the title someone had pencilled "Mrs Craik". I couldn't help but wonder if Mrs Craik was known for her unkind words, so much so, perhaps, that a previous reader had instinctively added her name on seeing the title.

As the story had been published in the mid-1800s, I could be pretty sure the lady in question was long departed from this life, and I thought it a terribly sad way to be remembered.

"It just emphasises the importance," I said to myself, "of living and speaking in such a way that, if we are remembered at all, it will be kindly."

A little research proved that Dinah Craik was, in fact, the author of the story. I did feel foolish for a moment, but I think the point still stands.

November

CAROL-ANNE believes in God. Her husband doesn't. But he's a good dad, so when his four-year-old son had nightmares and asked Dad to pray with him, he saw that it helped and he joined in. He just avoided the beginning and end, and any mention of God.

When the little fellow told his mum that Daddy believed in God, Carol-Anne pointed out that Daddy never used that name.

"I noticed that," the little fellow said, "but it's all right. God knows who he's talking to."

Monday — November 2

WE can look at the work of the potter as creating things – vases, plates, bowls, jugs.

Another way to look at it is that he or she creates useful spaces – spaces for storage, for flowers, for food, water and milk. Useful spaces. Spaces where things can be kept safe.

The material that makes us, our "clay" if you like, is already here, already ours to use. Now, what sort of useful safe spaces shall we create today?

Tuesday — November 3

IN Zakopane in Poland, there is a valley that used to be blocked by snow in winter. People found their own ways to deal with it.

They could have ignored it, but instead, when it was cold enough, they cut the snow into blocks and created a maze the size of several football pitches.

What had been a no-go area is now a tourist attraction.

As with so many things in life, the difference between a negative and a positive is a little imagination. Isn't that amazing?

The work of the potter is to create useful spaces.

Wednesday — November 4

A CHURCH organist gained a fine reputation – and a fine conceit of himself! He was for ever talking of the magnificent tunes he played. One day, the bellows-boy popped out from behind the organ and suggested the credit might be shared a little. The organist refused.

The next Sunday, the organist announced to the congregation, "Today, I shall be playing 'Sing O Heavens'." He put his fingers to the keys and nothing happened. From the front pew, the bellows-boy asked, "I? Or we?"

The desperate organist quickly reworded his announcement and the boy went to work. Together, they played beautiful music!

In a world of increasing interdependency, shall it be "I" or "we"?

Thursday — November 5

A MERICAN polymath Benjamin Franklin designed a coin bearing the motto *Mind your business*. What denomination was it? It was a one-cent coin. How much impact could a cent have on anyone's business? Perhaps it was a take on the British saying, "Take care of the pennies and the pounds will take care of themselves."

The same philosophy applies in health, relationships and education. The little things are important. In life as well as in business!

Friday — November 6

A NDREW is a retired carpenter, and he's busier now than he ever was. Why? Well, while he was working, his focus was on bringing in the money. He would do first-class work for his customers, and was always in demand.

Just as the cobbler's children went unshod, any work he did around the house tended to be slap-dash, so he could get back to his "real" work. Now he is having to undo all that and do it again properly.

"There's an old saying carpenters use," Andrew told me. "It's 'measure twice and cut once'. If I had measured the time I spent on work at home properly and valued it more, I would have got away with doing the work once, and be putting my feet up now!"

Saturday — November 7

WINTER can be bleak, but it can also be breathtaking!
In his book "In The Catskills", the American naturalist John Burroughs wrote that "he who marvels at the beauty of the world in summer will find equal cause for wonder and admiration in winter."

What he described as "the pomp and pageantry" – the flowers, the leaves – have been swept away, but the mountains and valleys are still there, as is the procession of day and night, the "infinite sky", the apparently rekindled stars, and so on.

Spring, summer, autumn or winter, it's a wonderful world regardless!

Sunday — November 8

STEVEN SPIELBERG is something of a cinematic genius. And "Schindler's List" is destined to be an all-time classic film. But, dealing with concentration camps and the Holocaust as it does, it is very depressing.

Which is why, popular legend has it, the comedian Robin Williams used to call Spielberg up during the filming and tell him jokes.

The most important tasks in life are often the most difficult. We need "doers" to make them happen, but we also need encouragers to make sure the "doers" don't give up.

In this life, be one or the other.

Monday — November 9

WHAT did you do with the core of the last apple you ate? Throw it away? Compost it? Take out the seeds and plant them?

An apple usually has around five seeds inside it. Imagine each one grew into a tree. Imagine if each tree produced a hundred apples in its lifetime. That's two thousand and five hundred seeds. And so on.

Now, imagine a smile or a kind deed was a seed. Because they, too, have the ability to create more like themselves.

What are you going to do with yours?

IN 1864, the English philosopher and writer Isaac Taylor wrote his definition of a family. In his opinion it might be husband and wife, brother and sister, son and daughter, or any combination thereof, provided they were "bound together by affection, esteem, respect and unaffected regard for each." A family, he allowed, might be as few as two people, "provided they are one in unselfish attachment."

We might have expanded our notions of what constitutes a family these days. But the bonds that hold that marvellous unit together will still be the same.

Wednesday — November 11

THE Spirit Of Man" is a compilation of writings; words Robert Bridges thought represented the best of humanity.

I glanced through it one day, looking for some thoughts on Remembrance Day, but I was surprised to find none. Then I realised that the book was published in 1916 – before there ever was such a day!

I wondered: will there ever come a time when we no longer have a Remembrance Day? I hope not. But a day when there are no new names added to the list of the glorious dead, that is something to be earnestly prayed for.

Thursday — November 12

THE foodbank was giving out children's books alongside the usual essential supplies. Someone (apparently in a position to be critical) questioned the gifts as a waste of resources.

One of the volunteers responded, "You didn't read when you were a child, did you? Or you would know a book is the quickest way to a place where you aren't hungry, where you aren't cold, where your family is together, and every story has a happy ending."

I watched the critic puff himself up. His face went red, then he turned and stomped out of the room.

Bless his heart, he came back two hours later with a bag of books!

Friday — November 13

MANDY looked at the puddle, wondering how to get across it. She wiped rain from her eyelashes and looked up.

A little boy looked out of a bus window. He smiled – the kind of innocent smile that goes straight to the heart – and waved.

"In that moment," she told me, "I wasn't just someone getting soaked. I was part of something. A family. Something bigger, perhaps. I stepped into that puddle wearing his smile. And didn't mind!"

Saturday — November 14

I'D never met him before, but he wanted to tell me how there was no good in the world any more: no honesty, no decency, and so on.

After twenty minutes of polite listening, I attempted to change the subject by asking where he was going next.

"Back into the shop," he said. "They gave me too much in my change. I don't want the cashier having to make it up at the end of her shift."

In a world where he believed there was no decency or honesty, he – perhaps without even realising it – was being decent and honest.

If we think the world is lacking something, and if we care enough about that something, we should be it. Then the world won't be lacking in it any more.

Sunday — November 15

IN winter, the Grüner See is a park with a large pond in the middle. There are picnic benches, pathways and views of the snow-covered Hochschwabb mountains.

In spring, all that snow starts to melt and run downhill. By mid-summer the park is a lake, up to forty feet deep, and its crystal-clear water makes it a big attraction for scuba divers who can then swim above the picnic benches and walkways.

In winter, the lake barely exists. In summer, the park can hardly be found. But each is wonderful in its own season!

THE emperor-philosopher Marcus Aurelius observed the difference between those who thought themselves a part of a society and those who thought of themselves as members of the same society.

The difference was not in the words, nor in the works, but in the attitudes and the rewards.

Some did their duty "barely, as a thing of propriety". They did their duty. They could not be faulted. They earned their place.

Yet Marcus Aurelius thought they missed out. Those who did the same things but "delighting in love and kindness for its own sake" benefited not only others, but also themselves. With no extra effort.

If we would, or must, be a part of something, may we – especially on Monday mornings – put our whole heart into it. For everyone's sake.

TWO hundred years ago, Maria Magdalena Matisdottir was a reindeer herder in Lapland. She told a British correspondent that it was often dark before the reindeer were brought to safety.

Then, exhausted, she would "lie down on the snow to sleep, and thank God that we had it to rest upon."

What's the point I'm making? No point at all! I just hope, with that image in mind, you sleep a little cosier in your bed tonight.

IF I could hold this sunset
And melt it in a pot,
If I could capture moonbeams
And tie them in a knot;
If I could pierce the storm clouds
And lure the hidden sun,
Then light would last for ever
And dark would be undone.

Patsy Goodsir

MUM had arrived home and the babysitter was recounting how the children had been. She mentioned that three-year-old Evie had indulged in one epic tantrum but been fine the rest of the day.

Evie explained, "I grumpy because I tired. I sorry. I have nap. I better now." Then she toddled off to play with her dolls.

"More grown-ups should be that self-aware," the baby-sitter said.

"So easily done, yet so effective," Mum added.

Many of us, regardless of age, will be prone to our own version of tantrums. We could learn a lot from the wisdom of a three-year-old.

Friday — November 20

IN a park in Turin is a sculpture that looks like two old-fashioned lampposts having a seat on a bench.

Looking at it, I thought about the people who shine lights of positivity, optimism and love into our lives. Most of them aren't like that "just because". Usually they have experienced the darkness, and know the importance of the light – for everyone.

They shine a little brighter for those who can't, and for those who need it. But it takes its toll.

The lights in our lives deserve every break, every encouraging word, every chance to sit down that we can give them, so they can keep on shining!

Saturday — November 21

DEFOREST KELLEY would never have become as famous had his original career path worked out. He wanted to be a doctor, but couldn't afford medical school. Instead, he became known world-wide as the physician on the USS Enterprise: Star Trek's Doctor McCoy.

His proudest moments were when fans told him his portrayal of the ship's chief medical officer inspired them to become doctors.

We don't all get to walk the paths in life we would choose, but if we make the best of the path life chooses for us, we might be surprised where it takes us.

NORMAN MACLEOD, who was one of Queen Victoria's chaplains, described it as the decisive question of the Bible. What was it?

Simply this: "Wilt thou be made whole?"

All too often we think of religion as a set of restrictions – the "thou shalt nots"! But Jesus made the lame man walk, the blind man see, the bleeding woman healthy, the dead live. He took away sins and promised a life beyond this one. None of that was for his good. All of it has the potential to make us better – make us more whole.

The question still remains: "Wilt thou?"

Monday — November 23

NO matter how early I leave the house to collect the morning paper, I generally meet our dear friend Mary on the way.

The paths were full of puddles after some torrential rain the previous day, and the sun hadn't yet lightened the sky as far as we could see. Perhaps the birds on the treetops had a better view.

Forbearing to criticise me as a slugabed, she cupped her ear with her hand. I tuned my ears to try to hear what she heard.

"You know," she said, "it doesn't matter what sort of day yesterday was. The birds always start the new day with a song."

Walking on, I managed to refrain from singing, but I did give a little whistle!

Tuesday — November 24

ONE cold day, Harry reminded me of the old Scottish saying, "A poor seat might make a rich warming".

"When I was a boy," he recalled, "the 'poor' seat was a wooden bench, big enough for the bottoms of two brothers – if they were getting on! Mother and Father had the high-backed chairs, one either side of the coal fire. They were more comfortable than our poor stool, but they were to the sides of the fire and slightly above it. We were in front of the fire, and on the same level."

The humble position truly brings its own rewards.

Start each new day
with a song.

WINTRY November has come round to stay
Don't worry that it will bring dark, dreary days
Perhaps like the fifth there'll be fireworks and sparks,
Excitement and colour to brighten our hearts.
A dull day, or one with a crisp, cold bright sun,
A day for reflection or one filled with fun.
We can't ever know what tomorrow will bring,
A sorrow, or joy that will make our soul sing.
Live life to the full and don't worry ahead
"For I'm with you always," our Lord Jesus said.

Linda Brown

Thursday — November 26

ARTHUR RUBENSTEIN was told from an early age that his piano-playing ability was miraculous. He saw things differently.

"To be alive, to be able to walk, to see – those are miracles. I have adopted the technique of living life from miracle to miracle."

We can't all play piano, but we can all follow Rubenstein's example and live from miracle to miracle. In fact, we all do!

Friday — November 27

BEFORE the Industrial Revolution began, the majority of the population lived in the countryside. With plenty of space! With mass migration into the cities and towns for work, a new sort of creature was born. The next-door neighbour!

An essay written in the mid-1800s described the new neighbour as someone who must leave behind notions of rough self-dependence and "do unto others as he would be done by, give and take, and study the greatest happiness of the greatest number". If he, or she, did this, they would be counted a good neighbour.

If you are a next-door neighbour, remember it has not always been so. Once upon a time people needed instruction in the art.

If you have managed this without reading any "how-to" essays, then you must be a very good neighbour indeed!

AN old tale recalls a hungry woman meeting a child who holds an apple in each hand. The woman tells the girl she is hungry. The girl takes a bite out of one hand, then a bite out of the other.

The woman, annoyed at such selfishness, is about to berate her, when the girl holds out the apple in her right hand and says, "This one is the sweetest. Take it." There was kindness in the act that might have been blown away and counted for nothing had the woman's anger been swift.

Be quick to resort to thanks and praise, but take your time before responding in hurt and anger.

Sunday — November 29

HE helps with lots of church activities, but never attends services. "I hang around until I feel it having an effect on me," he said, "then I back away." He enjoys his bad habits and isn't ready to risk losing them.

A comedian-turned-actor was asked in a radio interview if he missed doing stand-up comedy. He said he didn't miss hearing a news story and wondering what his cynical take on it could be. Not doing that had been great for his mental health.

They both knew – but only one was ready to accept – what the Apostle Paul was talking about when he advised us to focus on "whatever is noble, whatever is right, whatever is pure."

It wasn't for his sake, nor yet for God's, but for our good.

Monday — November 30

AS well as crafting some of the greatest novels American literature ever produced, and a fine collection of witticisms, Mark Twain also "discovered" what he believed to be a cure for bigotry, prejudice and narrow-mindedness.

He believed it also promoted "broad, wholesome and charitable views of men and things".

What was this wonderful medicine? Travel!

Excitement and colour
to brighten our hearts.

December

FOR a while I had an expensive camera (using old-fashioned 35 mm film) and people would admire my albums, praising my photographic skills.

What they didn't see were the many snaps that were "filed" in the bin. My collections were good because I vetted what people got to see. Folk do the same on social media these days.

Imagine if we didn't have to. If all our photos were works of art, if every aspect of our lives could happily be presented to the world. Well, I can't help with the first part, but as for the second part . . .

For a life that's worth living – and showing – may I recommend some advice I, coincidentally, saw on the cover of a photo album? It was a quote from 1 Corinthians and it said, "Let all that you do be done in love." Imagine living like that!

Then we wouldn't need to hide anything away, and we could take as many pictures of it as we liked.

Wednesday — December 2

IN "Resolution And Independence", the poet William Wordsworth talks of a period of despondency which was dispelled after meeting an old man who endured the trials of his rough life patiently.

In one line of the poem he writes, "The rain came heavily and fell in floods." A few lines later, he adds, "And all the air is filled with pleasant noise of waters."

The old man's fortitude would never have been the result of an easy life. Wordsworth's uplifting poem might never have been written without that downturn in his feelings.

Gurgling streams rarely come about without heavy rain. And without those "down" days we would not appreciate the good ones nearly as much.

Thursday — December 3

MUCH of the world knows the legend of the little Dutch boy who saved his town, and the low-lying countryside around it, by plugging a hole in the sea wall with his finger. Mostly, we remember his heroism in staying there all night long until help arrived.

But he would never have discovered that hole if he hadn't been on an errand for his mother, taking fresh-baked cakes to a blind man who lived at the other end of the wall.

In real life (as in this story), heroes rarely spring fully formed into the world's gaze. Often, they are formed in the kindnesses and wisdom of other people – usually mothers and fathers – whose deeds are rarely remembered by history.

Next time you read of someone doing some wonderful thing, spare a thought for those who taught them such a thing might be possible and that they could do it.

Friday — December 4

A FRIEND was a bit fed up with her life. She wanted more from it; more depth, more beauty. So she joined a writing group!

I confessed I thought it an unusual response. She explained she had been reading the Austrian poet Rainer Maria Rilke, who said, "If your daily life seems poor, do not blame it; blame yourself, tell yourself that you are not poet enough to call forth its riches; for to the Creator there is no poverty."

"It occurred to me," she said, "that my life already had everything necessary for a good story and I just had to learn to write it better."

I look forward to "reading" her next chapter.

Saturday — December 5

THE American banker and industrialist J.P. Morgan once said, "A man always has two reasons for doing anything: a good reason and the real reason."

I would not wish to cast aspersions on the motives of millionaires, but I would suggest a good man has one reason for his actions. His "good reason" and his "real reason" will be the same.

Sunday — December 6

ACCORDING to an old fable, the mountain once started groaning in pain, as if it were in labour. People gathered from miles around to see what would be produced. After a huge upheaval, the mountain gave birth to a mouse.

Now, some people might say life's like that: a lot of effort often produces a small return. Others might say that we underestimate the miracle that is a mouse and the value of the little things.

Monday — December 7

BECAUSE they often accompany unhappy situations, we think of tears as bad things. But there is more to them. An experimental photographer took microscopic images of tears cried in different situations and found they had very different compositions.

We cry at beauty, we cry when afraid, or when onions irritate our eyes. We associate tears with the things that cause them, but neglect the gifts they bring; the cleansing, the healing, the washing away of draining emotions.

Is it any wonder the Psalmist was sure God listed our tears and kept them? Those little drops are precious things indeed.

Tuesday — December 8

LET Christmas work its magic beneath the frosty sky,
As snowflakes gently drift to earth – let your spirit fly.
Rest here in the moment, beside the glittering trees;
Listen out for reindeer bells with childlike fun and glee.
Don't worry about days to come, life has its special way
Of working out our problems as we travel through each day.
Trust in the Christmas story you've often heard before
And tiptoe very quietly to the open stable door.
In your heart, you'll see him, that little baby boy,
Then deep within you'll know a peace beyond all earthly joy.
Your heart will sing for Christmas with the angels, pure and true,
As heaven and earth are joined by God's son, born for you.

Marian Cleworth

A frosty morning landscape, full of beauty.

North Yorkshire Moors National Park.

MOST people will have heard of the taxman. Fewer will know the term "tacksman".

In days gone by, in the Scottish Highlands, a tacksman would rent land from the laird and then sub-let parts of it. So, he might seem like a tenant and a landlord, but he was oft-times much more than that.

Usually the most educated man in any district – an English tourist recalled conversing with one in Gaelic, Latin and French, before settling on English as a common tongue – the tacksman was seen as a boon to the working folk. World affairs and the latest farming techniques would generally be heard first from him.

Samuel Johnson, the lexicographer, wrote, "If the tacksmen be abolished, who will be left to impart knowledge or impress civility?"

Of course, there were good and bad, but the tacksmen were generally a force for improvement.

If only more people would be less taxing and more like the tacksman.

AN artist friend of mine had planned to take a winter holiday in a sunnier climate, but she lost her passport and therefore couldn't go.

So, she stayed at home instead.

Was she sad about missing the holiday? Yes, of course.

Did she mope? No.

Instead, she created an animation of a cold and windy street – the very street that she lived on. Then she had the camera draw back, revealing the fact that the entire street was on a boat, sailing for tropical lands.

If we can create something positive even from our disappointments, then what can stop us?

(And the money she earned from the animation paid for an even better holiday!)

Friday — December 11

EDWARD ROWLAND SILL, a poet and educator in the nineteenth century, wrote a poem in which a king, jokingly, asked a jester for a prayer.

Hamming it up, the jester recounted the King's failings, pretending they were his own. After each, he said, "Be merciful to me, a fool."

Everyone expected the King to fly into a rage. Instead, he took a walk in his garden where he could be heard muttering, "Be merciful to me, a fool."

None of us know it all or can do it all. Until we do and until we can, let us remember to be humble.

Saturday — December 12

WE age, inevitably. But need we lose touch with our youth? Robert Louis Stevenson, the author of "Treasure Island", suggested we still have a path in our souls connected to our youth. He wrote, "Grandfather William can retire upon occasion into the green, enchanted forest of his boyhood."

Perhaps that path has become overgrown and impassable. Can I recommend secateurs?

Sunday — December 13

WOULD you like to know what heaven is like before you get there? The Christian writer and author of the Narnia books, C.S. Lewis, gave the matter a lot of thought and decided that he wouldn't. Why not?

Well, he decided that if he knew what it was like, he would also know that it wasn't any better than that. As creative as his mind obviously was, Lewis knew that his imagination was limited by his human experience. God, he understood, had no such limitations, and so would have created an eternal home wonderful beyond anything we could possibly dream of.

So, what will heaven be like? Imagine the best. Then rest assured that it will be better. Much better!

Monday — December 14

BOBBY shook my hand and said, "Thank you."

When I said I didn't know what he was talking about, he explained. Friends and family had clubbed together to help him with something. But some chose to help anonymously.

"So, rather than miss them out," he said, "I'm just thanking everyone I can think of."

To my protest that I hadn't helped, he added, "But you have before, or you will at some time, so nothing is lost by thanking you anyway."

Thanking everyone you meet for help given in the past, the present, or in the future – there's a lesson in gratitude I was thankful to receive.

Tuesday — December 15

HE was playing a Dungeons and Dragons game with his daughters. Their online personas were in a village surrounded by hungry wolves.

While he tried to figure out a way to defeat them or a way to escape, his daughters fed the wolves and turned them into a friendly army.

Before you settle for anyone being an enemy, make sure you have tried every way available to make them a friend.

Wednesday — December 16

HE looked like he lived a rough life. I knew he wasn't having a good day because I'd heard him arguing with his boss before he climbed into the cab of his truck.

I was standing beside a lad of five, whose eyes widened and jaw dropped as he saw the giant gravel-laden dump-truck drive by. The man looked out, gave a toot of the horn, and made the lad's day.

Bless his heart, I thought. No matter how difficult his path through life has been, he still remembers what it is to be an innocent little boy.

Thursday — December 17

THE 13th-century poet, Rumi, has probably never been more popular, even though he died more than 700 years ago!

His verses on the nature of man and his relationship with his creator can be found on posters and cards and are all over the internet.

Like King Solomon in the Bible, Rumi often referred to God as his "beloved".

"To find the beloved, you must become the beloved."

He died on this day in 1273, but the day is not remembered in his homeland as a sad one.

Instead, it is referred to as his wedding night: the time when he was reunited with his beloved, his creator; his love above all loves.

Friday — December 18

IT was raining heavily one day, and we had just returned home from an outing.

Standing on the doorstep, I attempted to unlock the front door, but the key wouldn't turn.

The more frustrated I became, the harder I twisted the key, and the more it stayed stuck!

"Why don't you try?" I suggested to the Lady of the House beside me, feeling rather exasperated. "Perhaps I'm not holding the key right."

"You are holding the key just fine," she assured me with a small smile. "Perhaps the problem is in how you are holding your mouth."

Too cold for riddles, I was tempted to be cross.

Then I thought I understood.

Understanding brought a smile to my face.

The smile relaxed me and the key turned.

I bowed, stepped back (still smiling), and let her in out of the rain first.

Santa's helper hopes
there's a bone inside!

THE American writer and philosopher Ralph Waldo Emerson was once accused of being too much of a rationalist and not enough of a romantic. He apologised – after a fashion.

He allowed that the experience of "a beauty, overpowering all analysis or comparison" often overcame those of thirty years of age and under.

Older people, he seemed to imply, had a more sober, considered view of the world.

But he did concede that the memories of such times tended to outlast all other remembrances and were "a wreath of flowers on the oldest brows."

There is such awe-inspiring beauty in life. And some of us enjoy it way past the age of thirty.

Whether we are experiencing it or remembering, we can never deny it. To do so – as Emerson, the great rationalist knew – would be extremely irrational!

WE hear a lot about keeping Christ in Christmas.

I was in a different church from usual recently and found myself sitting beside a beautiful nativity scene. From a side-on position, I could see, lying behind the stable, neglected and with arms reaching up, the Baby Jesus! The little manger was empty.

I wondered if the minister had hidden it there or if it had been some childish mischief. If I put it back, would I be spoiling some surprise the minister had set up?

In the end, I picked the little figure up and, with a silent prayer of thanks, I laid him in the manger.

The minister saw me and said, "Ah, I was wondering where our Lord was."

When it comes to keeping Christ in Christmas, it's not a case of railing against a secular society. It is much more of an individual, personal thing.

Do it for you, and for him. Keep the Lord in your heart and he will always be in Christmas.

CHRISTMAS. In a lot of ways, it makes no sense. It's a mix of traditions any reasoning man can pick apart and scoff at (if he had a heart of stone).

It's the nonsensical alongside the wonderful, the frivolous beside the deeply spiritual.

If we were to concern ourselves with the reason why we did the thing, we would do half as much – if that – of the things we traditionally do.

But, if it brings people together, if it adds to the joy of the world, does it really need to withstand serious enquiry?

As the American author Madeleine L'Engle once wrote, "Had Mary been filled with reason, there'd have been no room for the child."

Allow yourself the nonsense, the fun; blend as many traditions as you like if it increases the love – but, always, remember the child.

Tuesday — December 22

IN a 1902 edition of "The Hospital" newspaper, it was announced that there would, once again, be a collection of clothing and "useful articles" for those who would be residing in hospital that Christmas.

On this particular year, however, they planned to do things a little differently.

They would first display the collection for a few days before parcelling it out to the patients.

The intention was to "give an object lesson on what can be done by kind hearts and capable hands."

Showing off? Not at all. Encouraging others by opening their eyes to possibilities? Definitely.

"Kind hearts" rarely want their work publicised. That's not why they do what they do.

But, of course, there's no denying the publicity does help encourage other hearts to be kind as well.

THERE'S a lot of it around at this time of the year, and it's very infectious.

A group of primary one children – four- and five-year-olds – were walking in pairs from school to church for their Christmas service.

Holding hands wasn't enough for them: two of them started singing the song "Rudolph The Red-nosed Reindeer". It soon spread!

The children behind them joined in, then the children in front of them joined in, and finally the teachers and parent helpers joined in.

A woman walking past with her grandson caught it, and they both joined in. Who knows who they infected after that?

Christmas spirit. There's a lot of it about at this time of the year. And it's very infectious.

MY morning stroll started in a new housing development. The streets were empty.

Everyone will be out working to pay for these huge mortgages, I thought.

Then I entered a noticeably rougher, poorer area. A young man coming out to his car said hello to me and we chatted about the weather.

I walked on. In my head I was all set to make a philosophical point about how material wealth robs life of its quality time; about how poorer people are often nicer.

Imagine how frustrated I was when, back in the well-to-do area, a young woman leaving her house to walk her dog stopped for a chat with me – and was just as friendly and pleasant as the man had been!

There was no lesson to be learned there, then.

Except, perhaps, that whether people are friendly or otherwise will usually depend more on the size of their hearts than on the size of their houses.

IN "A Treasury Of The Familiar" Ralph L. Woods gathered a collection of fine speeches, touching poetry and excerpts from the Bible; pieces guaranteed to lift the spirits of the reader.

I opened it and a sheet of typed paper fell out. A previous reader had copied a poem by Walt Whitman and inserted it by the rear cover of the book.

I checked the index. That poem was nowhere to be found. So, the reader had taken a collection of literary jewels, enjoyed it (I assume), and then added another jewel.

Oh, that we should do the same as we walk through this life! Appreciating all it has to offer and leaving it a richer experience for those who come after.

Saturday — December 26

GOOD KING WENCESLAS looked out, on the Feast of Stephen." That is today!

Wenceslas wasn't actually a king; he was a duke of Bohemia. But when the carol mentions him taking food to the hungry and firewood to the cold, it is spot on. That's exactly the sort of thing the historical Wenceslas did, as a Christian who tried to live the teachings of Jesus. His life was such that he was considered for sainthood immediately after his death.

In the song, Wenceslas looks out from the comfort and security of his castle, sees a poor man gathering firewood in the snow and decides to help. If we have had a good Christmas – whether rich in material goods or in happiness – how better can we show our appreciation than by helping someone who had less?

If the song teaches us one thing, it is that our good deeds will have knock-on effects. His page-boy was freezing behind the "king" when he started walking in his master's footsteps. Miraculously, those footprints contained enough warmth to revitalise the boy.

Your good deed might set an example and warm hearts. Others might be helped because of it. Wenceslas's footsteps are well worth following in. As are those of his master.

Sunday — December 27

IF the weather is working as it always has – and, of course, there is no guarantee of that – we will soon be heading into a time of snow. The thought reminded me of the Lebanese-American poet Kahlil Gibran who wrote, "Kindness is like snow. It beautifies everything it covers."

There is no question but that a fresh blanket of snow smooths out all the bumps and helps the world to sparkle.

"Ah," the cynic might add, "but what about afterwards? What about all that unpleasant slush?"

Well, that's where kindness wins over snow. Snow has its season and must eventually be washed away. But there is no "afterwards" with kindness; no reason why we can't keep on smoothing out bumps and helping the world to sparkle.

Monday — December 28

OUR friend Mary was on her way back from the shops. I couldn't help noticing the empty jar at the top of her shopping bag.

"You bought a jar of nothing?" I asked.

"I think of it as a jar of possibilities," she told me. "Each day, I plan to write something good that happened. Then, at the end of next year, I shall sit down with a cuppa and enjoy those precious memories." Her smile was replaced by a thoughtful expression.

"There are some who would fill this jar in a week, and some who wouldn't cover the bottom of it in a year. And, looking at their lives, you would never know which was which. Perhaps my first note should say I am thankful to be thankful."

Tuesday — December 29

STAMFORD'S "Art Of Reading" was a regular digest, published in Boston, Massachusetts, in the early 1800s. From that periodical come these words of advice, no less applicable today than then.

"Count that day lost whose low descending sun
Views from thy hand no worthy action done."

WHY is a bluebell so bonnie and blue;
Why is a buttercup gold?
Why is a blossom heartbreakingly pure;
What makes a snowdrop so bold?
How does an apple grow rosy and red
Or russet, or yellow, or green?
Why does a peach have a velveteen coat;
Why is a nettle so mean?
How do the bulbs, so snug in the earth,
Hear the light footfall of spring?
How do the feathered heralds of dawn
Learn all the songs that they sing?
Who gave every harlequin flower
Its very own personal scent?
Did all transpire by accident,
Or by Divine intent?
While questions wait for answers,
Sweet wisdom's inner voice
Whispers, "Feel the wonder, and
Rejoice, rejoice, rejoice."

Tricia Sturgeon

Thursday — December 31

THE ship, the SS *Ayrfield*, was built in 1911 and taken to the breakers' yard in 1972. The breakers went out of business, so the old hulk sat there, rusting and falling to bits in a bay that was heavily polluted.

But nature found a use for it and now the framework has a miniature forest of mangrove trees growing from it. The *Ayrfield* has become a tourist attraction and the mangroves are playing no small part in purifying the waters of the bay.

Nature often needs only the smallest toe-hold – the slightest opportunity – to start turning things around and making them better. May we be as imaginative, and as determined, when it comes to making those changes for the better – for us and the world around us – in the year ahead.

Let it snow, let it snow,
let it snow . . .